ABOUT THE AUTHORS

Dr. Wilfred Funk and Norman Lewis have both been deeply concerned with the history and use of the English language for many years. As editors, lexicographers, teachers and authors, they have each contributed extensively to this important field. But successful as they have each been individually, their success as collaborators in producing *30 Days to a More Powerful Vocabulary* has been even greater. In various editions, at various prices, this book has sold over 2,500,000 copies. It is the most popular and most widely used manual of its kind produced in the twentieth century.

WILFRED FUNK and NORMAN LEWIS

30 Days to
A MORE POWERFUL
VOCABULARY

WASHINGTON SQUARE PRESS, INC. · NEW YORK

30 Days to a More Powerful Vocabulary

Wilfred Funk edition published September, 1942

A *Washington Square Press* edition
1st printing.......................January, 1949
41st printing..........................June, 1963

This WASHINGTON SQUARE PRESS edition includes every word contained in the original, higher-priced edition. It is printed from brand-new plates made from completely reset, clear, easy-to-read type.

Published by   L

Washington Square Press, Inc.: Executive Offices, 630 Fifth Avenue; University Press Division, 32 Washington Place, New York, N.Y.

WASHINGTON SQUARE PRESS editions are distributed in the U.S. by Affiliated Publishers, a division of Pocket Books, Inc., 630 Fifth Avenue, New York 20, N.Y.

CONTENTS

vii

GIVE US 15 MINUTES A DAY

Your boss has a bigger vocabulary than you have.

That's one good reason why he's your boss.

This discovery has been made in the word laboratories of the world. Not by theoretical English professors, but by practical, hard-headed scholars who have been searching for the secrets of success.

After a host of experiments and years of testing they have found out:

> That if your vocabulary is limited your chances of success are limited.
>
> That one of the easiest and quickest ways to get ahead is by consciously building up your knowledge of words.
>
> That the vocabulary of the average person almost stops growing by the middle twenties.
>
> And that from then on it is necessary to have an intelligent plan if progress is to be made. No haphazard hit-or-miss methods will do.

It has long since been satisfactorily established that a high executive does not have a large vocabulary merely because of the opportunities of his position. That would be putting the cart before the horse. Quite the reverse is true. His skill in words was a tremendous help in getting him his job.

Dr. Johnson O'Connor of the Human Engineering Laboratory gave a vocabulary test to 100 young men who were studying to be industrial executives.

Five years later those who had passed in the upper ten per cent *all,* without exception, had executive positions, while *not a single young man of the lower twenty-five per cent had become an executive*.

You see, there are certain factors in success that can be measured as scientifically as the contents of a test-tube, and it has been discovered that the most common characteristic of outstanding success is "an extensive knowledge of the exact meaning of English words."

The extent of your vocabulary indicates the degree of your intelligence. Your brain power will increase as you learn to know more words. Here's the proof.

Two classes in a high school were selected for an experiment. Their ages and their environment were the same. Each class represented an identical cross-section of the community. One, the control class, took the normal courses. The other class was given special vocabulary training. At the end of the period the marks of the latter class surpassed those of the control group, not only in English, but in every subject, including mathematics and the sciences.

Similarly it has been found by Professor Emeritus Lewis M. Terman, of Stanford University, that a vocabulary test is as accurate a measure of intelligence as any three units of the standard and accepted Stanford-Binet I. Q. tests.

The study of words is not merely something that has to do with literature. Words are your tools of thought. *You can't even think at all without them.* Try it. If you are planning to go down town this afternoon you will find that you are saying to yourself: "I think I will go down town this afternoon." You can't make such a simple decision as this without using words.

Without words you could make no decisions and form no judgments whatsoever. A pianist may have the most beautiful tunes in his head, but if he had only five keys on his piano he would never get more than a fraction of these tunes out.

Your words are *your* keys for *your* thoughts. And the more words you have at your command the deeper, clearer and more accurate will be your thinking.

A command of English will not only improve the processes of your mind. It will give you assurance; build your self-confidence; lend color to your personality; increase your popularity. Your words are your personality. Your vocabulary is you.

Your words are all that we, your friends, have to know and judge you by. You have no other medium for telling us your thoughts—for convincing us, persuading us, giving us orders.

Words are explosive. Phrases are packed with TNT. A simple word can destroy a friendship, land a large order. The proper phrases in the mouths of clerks have quadrupled the sales of a department store. The wrong words used by a campaign orator have lost an election. For instance, on one occasion the four unfortunate words "Rum, Romanism and Rebellion" used in a Republican campaign speech threw the Catholic vote and the presidential victory to Grover Cleveland. Wars are won by words. Soldiers fight for a phrase. "Make the world safe for Democracy." "All out for England." "V for Victory." The "Remember the Maine" of Spanish war days was changed to "Remember Pearl Harbor" during World War II.

Words have changed the direction of history. Words can also change the direction of your life. They have often raised a man from mediocrity to success.

If you consciously increase your vocabulary you will unconsciously raise yourself to a more important station in life, and the new and higher position you have won will, in turn, give you a better opportunity for further enriching your vocabulary. It is a beautiful and successful cycle.

It is because of this intimate connection between words and life itself that we have organized this small volume in a new way. We have not given you mere lists of unrelated words to learn. We have grouped the words around various departments of your life.

This book is planned to enlist your active cooperation. The authors wish you to read it with a pencil in your hand, for you will often be asked to make certain notations, to write answers to particular questions. The more you use your pencil, the more deeply you will become involved, and the deeper your involvement the more this book will help you. We shall occasionally ask you to use your voice as well as your pencil—to say things out loud. You see, we really want you to keep up a running conversation with us.

It's fun. And it's so easy. And we've made it like a game. We have filled these pages with a collection of devices that we hope will be stimulating. Here are things to challenge you and your friends. Try these tests on your acquaintances. They will enjoy them and it may encourage them to wider explorations in this exciting field of speech. There are entertaining verbal calisthenics here, colorful facts about language, and many excursions among the words that keep our speech the rich, flexible, lively means of communication that it is.

Come to this book every day. Put the volume by your bedside, if you like. A short time spent on these pages before you turn the lights out each night is better than an irregular hour now and then. If you can find the time to learn only two or three words a day—we will still promise you that at the end of thirty days you will have found a new interest. Give us *fifteen minutes a day,* and we will guarantee, at the end of a month, when you have turned over the last page of this book, that your words and your reading and your conversation and your life will all have a new and deeper meaning for you.

For words can make you great!

TAKE THIS VOCABULARY TEST

First, we shall take your word portrait.

When the picture is finished it will show you how you look to others as a conversationalist and how you may appear when you write a simple social note or a business letter.

The lines of your likeness that are to be drawn here will indicate the extent of your vocabulary, the facility with which you can recall and use words, and the knowledge that you have of their precise meanings. There will also be two brief spelling and pronunciation tests so that we can get a complete picture.

You will find the tests in this chapter simple and entertaining. They will scarcely take you fifteen minutes to do. When you are through and have marked yourself, you will know what's wrong, if anything, with your vocabulary and your use of words. You will, in short, have painted your own word portrait. Then, in the chapters that follow, we will show you just how to strengthen any weak points that may have appeared.

How do words treat you, anyhow? Are you comfortable with them? Do they come easily to you? When you write and speak, do your words paint the sort of picture of you that will do you the most good in this highly competitive world? Does your language make you happy? Does it always hold a true mirror up to your mind, your emotions,

6

your personality, so that they may be properly reflected? Or does it sometimes betray you and blur your thoughts? Do people occasionally misunderstand you? Or can you compel them to listen, react, obey?

Like everyone else on this earth of ours you want certain definite things from life. No matter what those favors are, or what particular way you have chosen to go about getting them, you know that your first and most effective means will be the words you use.

Except for the gift of words no book, including this one, would ever be in your hands. You couldn't even read the title. Nor, having opened the covers, could you understand the contents. And you would thus be denied all the knowledge of the ages. In like manner the satisfaction and the success you hope to get out of life will depend very greatly on the skill with which you can communicate your needs, your desires, your opinions to the other humans who are around you.

What you say to others is important. A girl may be ever so beautiful, but once she speaks, she registers her class, and no expensive dress can cover her bad grammar or faulty pronunciation. Her words have made her homely. The late Lilyan Tashman, motion picture star of her day, had a favorite anecdote in this connection. She had been asked to go to a party by a distinguished member of the Hollywood colony. As her escort was slipping a luxurious fur wrap over the actress's shoulders he murmured, "You look as lovely as a Botticelli angel." "Whad'da ya mean, Botticelli? What's that?" said the girl. "I saw," said Miss Tashman, "a look of faint disgust flick into the man's eyes, and from that time on I made up my mind to do a bit of studying."

How sure are you that *you* know fine shades of meanings? It is most important that you should or your word portrait is going to be slightly out of focus. And those splendid ideas you have are going to be distorted when you try to project them on the minds of others.

You see, words have individualities of their own. They have form, color, personality. When you learn to know them they will become your slaves and will work for you whether you are young or old. Whether or not you've been through college, or high school, or even grammar school, you will find these lessons growing easier for you, chapter by chapter, as you go along.

Now we are ready for your portrait. Please follow the instructions carefully. Sit very still. When your picture is finished, we'll show it to you and you will see how your words look to the outside world.

Test I (Elementary)

HOW QUICK ARE YOU WITH WORDS?

Time 30 Seconds

Directions: Take out your watch. Now write in the blank space next to each of the words in the following list another word *that begins with S* and has a meaning directly opposite to the given word.

Example:	fast	slow
	sweet	sour
	buy	sell

Now time yourself. Thirty seconds is enough. *Don't forget, every word must begin with the letter S.* In all the following tests mark yourself wrong on such words as you fail to get in the time limit.

1. tall ....
2. north ....
3. happy ....
4. different ....
5. dangerous ....
6. big ....
7. dull ....
8. noisy ....
9. sit ....
10. receive ....

(Answers for all of these questions and those that follow will be given at the end of the chapter.)

You have just been tested for fluency.

The dictionary men call words of opposite meanings *antonyms,* but you don't have to remember that unless you want to. The important thing is, that you should have breezed through the list at high speed in less than thirty seconds with no hesitancy and no mistakes. If you had to think for more than an instant to recall the proper word, it is likely that you experience some discomfort in expressing your thoughts in your daily life. You are probably seeing men not as bright as you getting ahead of you. You may often wonder: "What has he got that I haven't got?"

Without the proper word arsenal you will have to resign yourself to mediocrity. You are seriously handicapped. But don't worry too much about it. Most people are. This book is designed for you. It will give you the chance to go to work and overcome your obstacle.

Test II—Verbal Speed (Advanced)

Time 90 Seconds

Directions: The principle is the same as in the last test. That is, write a word beginning with *S* which is opposite in meaning to each of the following. These answers of yours will be the *antonyms*. A minute and a half by your watch should be enough.

1. generous ....
2. meaningless ....
3. believing ....
4. complicated ....
5. doubtful ....
6. careful ....
7. wakefulness ....
8. rough ....

9. objective ....

10. laugh ....

Speed and accuracy are again of great importance. If you completed this in ninety seconds and got eight out of ten correct, you are far above the average and you doubtless show unusual skill and ease in translating your thoughts into the proper words; you are going to make swift progress in the lessons that are ahead.

If, on the other hand, you exceeded your time limit, or if you were wrong in five or more words, it is critically necessary that you should start in today to improve your fluency. We are dealing, in this book, with the richest language in the world, and with a little practice and patience you can easily make its great power belong to you.

Test III

HOW ARE YOUR SYNONYMS?

Time 4 Minutes

We now want to test your skill from another point of view. You have tried the antonyms, or words of opposite meanings. How will you do with synonyms, or words of the same, or almost the same, meanings? It is highly important that you have a wealth of synonyms at your command. They are like the many colors on an artist's palette. They will help you paint in for others the many shades of thoughts that are in your mind.

Directions: In the spaces given below write two words that are synonymous with the given word.

> *Example:* beautiful   lovely, pretty
> strong   rugged, powerful
> short   brief, concise

This test should be finished within the time limit, as there are many more than two synonyms for each of these words. There will be very few times, in this book, that you will have to refer to a dictionary. It may be necessary, however, in this test, to check in case your answers do not sufficiently agree with those given at the end of the chapter.

Clock yourself for speed. You should finish this in four minutes or less.

1. defects   ....
2. desires   ....
3. true   ....
4. suitable   ....
5. luminous   ....
6. loathing (*noun*)   ....
7. doubtful   ....
8. vulgar   ....
9. admiration   ....
10. very   ....

This subject of synonyms that we have just touched upon is extremely important. The ability to call upon a variety of synonyms gives flexibility and depth to your writing and to your conversation.

TEST IV (SYNONYMS)

Time 80 Seconds

We have tested your ability to recall the synonyms for a given word. We are now going to test your ability to *recognize* synonyms when you see them.

Directions: In the following jumbled list there are sixteen words. Start with *infidel* and put a small figure 1 above it. Run through the list until you find another word that has the same or a similar meaning. Put a 1 beside it. Then try the second word on the list, *ingenious,* putting a figure 2 beside it and search for a word of similar meaning and mark it 2. And so on until you have eight pairs of synonyms or words of similar meaning. Try to finish this in eighty seconds.

infidel	ingenious	occur	aberration
large	happen	persuade	kidnap
bulky	eccentricity	clever	unbeliever
abduct	unsophisticated	induce	ingenuous

You can see, as we go along, how line by line is being added to your word portrait. And any flaws that are showing up are a warning to you that you are unnecessarily handicapped.

Test V

how are your homonyms?

Time 1 Minute

Homonyms are words that are pronounced exactly alike but mean different things. Let's test you on the meanings of a few such words. They are likely to be slightly confusing.

Directions: Here are five pairs of words. Fit each one of them into its proper place in the sentences. In the first sentence, for instance, both *alter* and *altar* must be used. The trick is, which word goes correctly in which blank space?

1. *Alter—altar*
   The bride wanted to .... her dress before the bridegroom took her to the ....

2. *gait—gate*
   The horse had a graceful .... as it trotted through the ....

3. *principle—principal*
   The .... of the High School was a dishonest man without a single ....

4. *capitol—capital*

   He went to Washington, the .... of the United States,
   and visited the beautiful .... building.

5. *complement—compliment*

   The owners of the ship could hardly help but ....
   the captain who had so swiftly gotten his full ....
   of men.

There are a surprising number of English words of this
type, that have the same sound, usually with a slight varia-
tion in spelling, but radically differ in meaning. Other
similar ones are: *stationary—stationery; raise—raze; aisle
—isle; rite—right; die—dye; bridal—bridle*. A knowledge
of these distinctions will be an important part of your
verbal equipment.

Test VI

DO YOU KNOW WHAT THESE WORDS MEAN?

Time 1 Minute

This will present some difficulties to those who have not
more than a fair grounding in the English language. A
few of these words are common. Some of the others are
known by only about fifty per cent of people. Two or
three are known to less than ten per cent. Try them and
see how you come out.

Directions: Let's start with *abject*. Reading across the
           page you will find three words given under

a, b and c. Check which one of these means the same thing as *abject*. Continue through the remaining nine words. This is a 60-second test.

1. *abject*
   a. downcast   b. refuse   c. ridiculous

2. *badinage*
   a. slavery   b. banter   c. equipment

3. *cadaver*
   a. corpse   b. attempt   c. knowledge

4. *ennui*
   a. anger   b. sorrow   c. boredom

5. *facetious*
   a. joking   b. cruel   c. useless

6. *incisive*
   a. doubtful   b. sharp   c. tooth

7. *maelstrom*
   a. flood   b. whirlpool   c. labyrinth

8. *nomad*
   a. maniac   b. fanatic   c. wanderer

9. *phlegmatic*
   a. temper-   b. placid   c. sick
      amental

10. *maudlin*
    a. supersen-   b. obscure   c. unusual
       timental

Test VII

HOW WELL CAN YOU SPELL?

No time limit

In the following paragraph check the words that have been spelled incorrectly, and write in your corrections.

We had a commitee meeting yesterday at our old adress to determine the number of bankrupcy cases on the calender and to assay both the debters and the defecit. It would be hard to discribe the embarassing situation that developed over our saleble securities, our pending forclosures and our promisory notes. In the end we decided it would be alright to put off all except the indespensable things until the Febuary meeting. (Would you say that some of these words are mispelled or misspelled?)

Test VIII

HOW WELL DO YOU PRONOUNCE?

No time limit

Many people have trouble with the pronunciation of the words in italics given below. Remember how *you* interpret them so you can check and mark yourself.

Jane had an *appendectomy*. Her *stamina* was good, although the whole *lamentable* affair was a *poignant* experience. For a brief time *peritonitis* threatened. But her *obese* and jolly doctor used careful hygiene and smart *psychiatry* on her and in the end Jane had enough *tenacity* to pull her through. Immediately upon her recovery Jane met a man who was not a *misogynist* and being no *misogamist* herself, they were married.

Now you may relax. Your word test is done. Your picture is finished. What you will see on the canvas—pleasant or unpleasant—is what the world sees when you write or when you speak. Please total your scores in the answer column that follows, see which group you belong in, and we shall then be ready to analyze your portrait for you.

ANSWERS   *Totals*

Test I   1. short 2. south 3. sad 4. same 5. safe
            6. small 7. smart or sharp 8. silent or still
            9. stand 10. send

            In scoring yourself allow 2 points for every
            correct word. Write your total at the right; 20
            would be perfect. Any answers written in after
            the time in any test must be considered wrong.   ....

Test II   1. selfish, stingy 2. sensible, significant 3. skep-
            tical 4. simple 5. sure 6. slipshod, slovenly,
            sloppy 7. sleep, sleepiness, slumber, somnolence
            8. smooth 9. subjective 10. sob

            Count 2 points for each correct answer. Per-
            fect score 20.   ....

Test III   1. shortcomings, imperfections, faults, weak-
            nesses, deficiencies, blemishes
            2. wishes, wants, longings, cravings, appetites
            3. right, correct, truthful, genuine, straight,
            honest, faithful, veracious, pure

ANSWERS *(Continued)* *Totals*

Test III 4. appropriate, consistent, fitting, fit, applicable

5. bright, lustrous, radiant, brilliant, vivid, gleaming, shining, glowing, lucid

6. disgust, aversion, detestation, antipathy, repugnance, abhorrence

7. ambiguous, vague, obscure, indefinite, loose, uncertain, dubious, questionable

8. rude, common, coarse, gross, ill-bred, low

9. praise, approval, commendation, esteem, veneration, approbation

10. extremely, exceedingly, highly, enormously, immensely, abundantly

Count 2 points for each question answered correctly. Failure to give 2 synonyms counts zero. Perfect score 20. ....

Test IV infidel, unbeliever; ingenious, clever; occur, happen; aberration, eccentricity; large, bulky; persuade, induce; kidnap, abduct; unsophisticated, ingenuous

Count 1 point for each word correctly paired. Total possible score, 16. ....

Test V 1. The bride wanted to *alter* her dress before the bridegroom took her to the *altar*.

2. The horse had a graceful *gait* as it trotted through the *gate*.

3. The *principal* of the High School was a dishonest man without a single *principle*.

4. He went to Washington, the *capital* of the United States, and visited the beautiful *Capitol* building.

ANSWERS (*Continued*)   *Totals*

Test V   5. The owners of the ship could hardly help
            but *compliment* the captain who had so
            swiftly gotten his full *complement* of men.

            Count 2 for each sentence you have correct.
            Perfect score, 10.   ....

Test VI   1-a; 2-b; 3-a; 4-c; 5-a; 6-b; 7-b; 8-c; 9-b; 10-a.

            Count 2 for each correct answer. Perfect score,
            20.   ....

Test VII   committee; address; bankruptcy; calendar;
            debtors; deficit; describe; embarrassing; sal-
            able; foreclosures; promissory; all right; indis-
            pensable; February; misspelled.

            Count 1 point for each word correctly spelled.
            Perfect score, 15.   ....

Test VIII   a-pen-dek'-toe-mee; stam'-in-a; lam'-en-ta-bul;
            poyn'-ant; pair-i-toe-nye'-tiss; o-beece'; sye-kye'-
            a-tree; te-nass'-i-tee; miss-oj'-i-nist; miss-og'-a-
            mist.

            Count 1 point for each word correctly pro-
            nounced. Perfect score, 10.   ....

110-131: If your score is 110 or above you belong up in the top
ten per cent of the literate population of this country and you
should be on the way to a high position in your vocational, intellectual, and social life. You will get a special pleasure out of
these lessons and you will be able further to perfect a vocabulary
that is already sound.

85-110: Your vocabulary is about average and is not helping you
to success as fast as it should. Why not begin today to overcome
this handicap? Start these lessons now and make this interesting

work a daily habit. The new words you learn will bring in new fields of knowledge to you, and there will be many subtle and indirect results. Mark this down in your book: There is no easier way to achieve success than by adding to your vocabulary.

85 and below: This mark shows a definitely impoverished vocabulary, and your weakness in words must have long since been holding you back. It would be a foolish and fatal mistake not to do something immediately about it. Here are three don'ts for you: Don't let your low mark unduly disturb you. Don't begin to think that "writers are born, not made." And don't feel that only a university graduate can be an expert user of words. Shakespeare attended school for ten years all told. Robert Burns, the Scotch poet, was a day laborer without education. Neither Charles Lamb nor Dickens had enough formal schooling to talk about. And Abraham Lincoln didn't know what the inside of a school looked like. They, and many others like them, became masters of speech. They achieved their effectiveness by industry and practice. So can you. And, when you do, your reward will be great.

The beauty of this book is that you start to benefit—not after months of trial—but from the first day and with the first chapter.

THE ROMANCE OF WORDS

From now on we want you to look at words intently, to be inordinately curious about them and to examine them syllable by syllable, letter by letter. They are your tools of understanding and self-expression. Collect them. Keep them in condition. Learn how to handle them. Develop a fastidious, but not a fussy, choice. Work always towards good taste in their use. Train your ear for their harmonies.

We urge you not to take words for granted just because they have been part of your daily speech since childhood. You must examine them. Turn them over and over, and see the seal and superscription on each one, as though you were handling a coin. *We would like you actually to fall in love with words.*

Words, as you know, are not dead things. They are fairly wriggling with life. They are the exciting and mysterious tokens of our thoughts, and like human beings, they are born, come to maturity, grow old and die, and sometimes they are even re-born in a new age. A word, from its birth to its death, is a process, not a static thing.

Words, like living trees, have roots, branches and leaves.

Shall we stay with this analogy for a few moments, and see how perfect it is?

The story of the root of a word is the story of its origin. The study of origins is called *etymology,* which in turn has *its* roots in the Greek word *etymon* meaning "true" and the Greek ending—*logia* meaning "knowledge." So *etymology* means the true knowledge of words.

Every word in our language is a frozen metaphor, a frozen picture. It is this poetry behind words that gives language its overwhelming power. And the more intimately we know the romance that lies within each word, the better understanding we will have of its meaning.

For instance, on certain occasions you will probably say that you have "calculated" the cost of something or other. What does this term "calculate" really mean? Here is the story. Years ago, ancient Romans had an instrument called a *hodometer,* or "road measurer," which corresponds to our modern taximeter. If you had hired a two-wheeled Roman vehicle to ride, say, to the Forum, you might have found in the back a tin can with a revolving cover that held a quantity of pebbles. This can was so contrived that each time the wheel turned the metal cover also revolved and a pebble dropped through a hole into the receptacle below. At the end of your trip you counted the pebbles and *calculated* your bill. You see the Latin word for pebble was *calculus,* and that's where our word "calculate" comes from.

There are, of course, many words with much simpler histories than this. When you speak of a "surplus," for instance, you are merely saying that you have a *sur* (French for "over") *plus* (French for "more") or a *sur-plus*. That is, you have an "over-more" than you need.

Should you be in a snooty mood for the nonce, and happen to look at someone rather haughtily, your friends might call you *supercilious,* a word which comes from the Latin *supercilium,* meaning that "eyebrow" you just raised.

That person you are so fond of, who has become your companion (*cum* [Latin for "with"] and *panis* [Latin for "bread"]), is simply one who eats bread with you. That's all. Again, "trumps" in bridge is from the French *triomphe* or triumph, an old-time game of cards. In modern cards one suit is allowed to triumph over, or to "trump" the other suits. And still again, in the army, the *lieutenant* is literally one who takes the place of the captain when the latter is not around. From the French *lieu* (we use it in "in lieu of") and *tenir,* "to hold." The captain, in turn, derives from the Latin word *caput* (head); colonel comes from *columna* (the "column" that he leads).

If, by any chance, you would like to twit your friend, the Wall Street broker, just tell him that his professional title came from the Middle English word *brocour,* a *broacher,* or one who opens, or broaches, a cask to draw off the wine or liquor. We still employ the same word in the original sense when we say "he broached (or opened up) the subject." Finally the broacher, or broker, became a salesman of wine. Then of other things, such as stocks and bonds.

These are the roots of words. We next come to the branches. The branches of our language tree are those many groups of words that have grown out from one original root.

Let's take an example. The Latin term *spectare* which means "to see" contains the root *spec,* and from this one root have sprouted more than 240 English words. We find the root hidden in such words as *spec*tacles, those things you "see" through; in re*spect,* the tribute you give to a person you care to "see" again; in*spect,* "to see" into; disre*spect (dis*—unwilling; *re*—again; *spec*—to see), therefore, when you treat someone with disrespect, you make it plain that you do not care to see him again; intro*spec*tion, looking or seeing within; *spec*tator, one who "sees" or watches.

Turning to the Greek language, which has so largely enriched our own, we discover the root appearing in English as *graph*. This means "to write" and has been a prolific source of words for us. We have tele*graph*, which literally means "far writing"; phono*graph*, "sound-writing"; photo*graph*, "light-writing"; steno*grapher*, one who does "condensed writing"; a *graph*ic description, one that is just as clear and effective as though it had been written down; mimeo*graph*, "to write a copy or imitation."

We have in our language a host of roots such as these. There is the Latin *spirare*, meaning "to blow or breathe," from which we get such English words as in*spire* (breathe into); ex*pire* (breathe out); per*spire* (breathe through); re*spir*ation (breathing again or often). And there is also our word "liable" that comes from the Latin *ligare*, "to bind." This fascinating root *lig* has branched out into ob*lig*e and ob*lig*ate (to bind to do something); *lig*ature (bandage or binding); *lig*ament (something that ties two things together); and, with the root no longer so obvious, "league" (those nations or other organizations that are bound together); and even the word "ally" which is from *ad* and *ligare*, to bind to one another.

These, then, are the branches. We turn now to the leaves. If the roots are the origins of words and the branches are the word families that stem out of them, the leaves of this language tree would be the words themselves and their meanings.

Each given word, in its beginning, had, no doubt, only

one meaning. But words are so full of life that they are continually sprouting the green shoots of new meanings.

Shall we choose just one word as an instance of the amazing vitality of language? The simple three letter word *run,* up to this moment of writing, has more than 90 dictionary definitions. There is the *run* in your stocking and the *run* on the bank and a *run* in baseball. The clock may *run* down but you *run* up a bill. Colors *run.* You may *run* a race or *run* a business or you may have the *run* of the mill, or, quite different, the *run* of the house when you get the *run* of things. And this little dynamic word, we can assure you, is not yet through with its varied career.

Is it any wonder that our unabridged dictionaries contain as many as 600,000 living and usable words, words sparkling with life, prolific in their breeding, luxuriant in their growth, continually shifting and changing in their meanings?

Words even have definite personalities and characters. They can be sweet, sour, discordant, musical. They can be sweet or acrid; soft or sharp; hostile or friendly.

From this time on, as we enter our word studies, try to become self-conscious about words. Look at them, if possible, with the fresh eyes of one who is seeing them for the first time. If we have persuaded you to do this, you will then be on the way to the success that can be won with a more powerful vocabulary.

WORDS FOR MATURE MINDS

There are words in this world of ours that can be understood only by those who have lived and become mature. No explanation, no definitions could make them clear to a child.

Here is such a list:

vicarious (vye-cair'-ee-us)
rationalize (rash'-un-al-ize)
gregarious (gre-gair'-ee-us)
obsequious (ob-see'-kwee-us)
maudlin (maud'-lin)

asceticism (a-set'-i-sizm)
pander (pan'-der)
sublimate (sub'-li-mate)
wanton (wahn'-ton)
effete (ef-feet')

The understanding of these words takes a certain amount of emotional maturity, and unless you have had certain experiences and emotional reactions you can have no comprehension of such words as these, because you have had no need for them.

You might find it hard, perhaps absolutely impossible, to explain the meanings of these terms to a twelve-year-old boy or girl.

But you, an adult, will be able to comprehend them and to make them your property.

Let's discuss them, one by one. Here and there we will

give you the etymology of the word, if its history is interesting and happens to throw any light on the present-day meaning.

1. *Vicarious:* This is an abstract word, but it is one that is easy for the grown-up mind to grasp. For example, there are two ways to travel. One, by buying a steamship ticket and going to your destination, say Havana. The other by reading travel stories or travel circulars *about* Havana. In the first instance you have enjoyed your travel experience *directly*. In the second instance you have enjoyed it *vicariously*.

A child is learning about life when he "pretends," when he plays "store," or "house," or "doctor." Of course he is fully living the life that children do, but he is also living adult life, not directly, but *vicariously*. And owing to his emotional immaturity, he is not ready, at his age, to grasp the difference, in thought and effect, between actual living and *vicarious* living. When he is older and more mature he will live less *vicariously* and more actually, and then he will be able to appreciate the significance of the word.

You, as an older person, will recognize that you are escaping from the real world and are living for the moment a *vicarious* existence and are having *vicarious* joys and sorrows when you are reading a book. You are living, not your own life, but the lives of the characters of the story. And the shop girl who haunts the movies can, for the time being, become the lovely, glamorous heiress to whom the hero makes the passionate love that she would like to experience herself. The screen is offering her *vicarious* thrills—substitutes for adventure, romance, travel, love. She is, for the time, living *vicariously*.

As an interesting sidelight, a vicar, who is a petty officer or assistant priest in the Church of England has delegated, but no direct, authority. Like *vicarious, vicar* comes from the Latin word *vicarius,* and both of them have inherited the same character of indirection.

2. *Rationalize:* You, as a human being, tend to *rationalize.* So do all of us. There are selfish men, for instance, who will never give anything to charity. They don't wish to regard themselves as selfish, however. They prefer to think that charity is harmful to the poor and demoralizes those who receive it. In this way the miser can save his money and his face at the same time. He is *rationalizing* his selfish act and the *rationalization* makes him feel better.

In similar fashion, a father who is angry may spank his boy merely to relieve his own personal feelings. But, in self-defense, he will *rationalize* his action by making himself believe that the spanking has been done for the good of the child.

The term *rationalize* has a number of meanings, but the most common one refers to the process of thought by which one justifies a discreditable act, and by which one offers to oneself and the world a better motive for one's action than the true motive.

3. *Gregarious:* This term comes from the Latin word *grex,* meaning a flock of cattle, and you know cattle like to stay together. If you are a *gregarious* type, you are a friendly person, a good mixer; you like to be with other people. That is, you are the extremely sociable kind. Because you are *gregarious* you enjoy parties, crowded theatres and dance floors; you like to be where folks flock in

small or large numbers. Because people are *gregarious,* they get married, have families, live in thronging cities, sing and play together. A hunger for love, friendship, and a feeling of kinship with other human beings is a normal and common human trait. It is a *gregarious* instinct.

4. *Obsequious:* The beggar, the underling, the lackey and the flunkey all tend to be *obsequious.* Those who wait on others in an inferior capacity and whose lives and jobs depend on the whims of their masters are apt to be cringing and fawning. They are often excessively, sickeningly and insincerely polite. If your waiter in a hotel or restaurant believes that you are the type who will tip him well, watch how *obsequious* he will be, how he will bow to you and attend on your slightest wish. If you *don't* leave the expected tip, his *obsequiousness* will quickly vanish and he will not (*ob,* "upon"; *sequor,* "follow") follow submissively upon your wishes.

5. *Maudlin:* A *maudlin* person is one who is supersentimental and gushing, who cries easily and without much cause. People who are *maudlin* in their affections usually overdo the act, and their love becomes tiresome and offensive. The word *maudlin* can also be applied to those who have been made foolish and silly by too much drinking.

Here, incidentally, is an odd word history. Mary Magdalene, who washed the feet of Christ, has often been pictured with her eyes red from weeping. As the centuries have gone by the proper name, Magdalene, has been contracted into the adjective, *maudlin.*

6. *Ascetic:* The *ascetic* is one who is given to severe self-denial and austerity and who practices rigid abstinence

and devotion, often to a religious cause. When you say that a man is an *ascetic,* you mean that he is one who shuns all the luxurious pleasures of life. Anyone who eats and drinks heartily or otherwise dissipates, is the precise opposite of an *ascetic,* and does not believe in *asceticism.*

7. *Pander:* This verb literally means to minister to the gratification of the passions and prejudices of others, usually to one's own profit. Many confession stories can be said to *pander* to the baser sex emotions. The yellow journals and the sensational press often *pander* to our love of crime. Ruthless dictators *pander* to the lowest instincts of the masses, to their selfishness, cruelty and greed, in order to gain power. *Pander,* therefore, is an unpleasant word with an unpleasant meaning. The noun *panderer,* has a still more restricted meaning, and frequently signifies a man who procures women for others, just as Pandarus, the leader of the Lycians in the Trojan war, is said to have procured the lovely lady Chryseis for Troilus.

8. *Sublimate:* This English word originally came from the Latin word *sublimatus,* which means "raised on high" and is closely related to our word "sublime." *Sublimate,* in its figurative sense, means to refine, to purify. Sometimes when the energies of the bad boy of the neighborhood are diverted into athletic games, or into a business career, or into some other channel of useful work, his former destructive activities are then said to have been *sublimated.* Again, psychologists tell us that lust and rapine, or the wish to persecute and kill, are often merely indications of excess energy. The majority of such people can be taught to *sublimate* these desires and passions in creative activities. This is *sublimation* in its highest and

most useful form, used in the sense of the original Latin word *sublimatus,* "raised on high."

9. *Wanton:* This old Anglo-Saxon term has many definitions, but when we say "he is a *wanton* man" we usually mean that he is a man who is living without restraint of appetite: especially one who is lecherous, lewd, lascivious and lustful.

10. *Effete:* When animals, plants or soil are worn out and incapable of producing, they are called effete (Latin *ex,* "out"; *fetus,* "having produced"). More commonly, though, this adjective is applied to man and to mankind. When, therefore, you are speaking of ancient Rome at the time of its fall and you characterize it as an *effete* civilization, you naturally mean that it was a civilization that was degenerate and completely worn out.

Now we want you to make these ten words your own possession and property. Below, in the column on the right, are the ten dictionary definitions of the words just discussed in this chapter. *They are not given in the order in which they appeared.* Take your pencil and try to fit each word to its proper definition.

1. .... tearfully sentimental

2. .... catering to evil desires

3. .... preferring the company of others to solitude

4. .... spent; exhausted; barren of energy; worn out by rich or effortless existence

5. .... one who practices extreme self-denial

6. .... enjoyed by one person through his sympathetic but indirect participation in the experience of another real or fictional person; substitutional

7. .... attributing one's actions to rational and creditable motives, without an adequate analysis of the true motives

8. .... servilely attentive; fawning

9. .... to direct energy from its primitive and destructive aim to one that is culturally or ethically higher

10. .... unchaste; lewd; also licentious. Marked by arrogant recklessness of justice, of the feelings of others, or the like; also having no just provocation; willfully malicious

ANSWERS: 1-maudlin; 2-pander; 3-gregarious; 4-effete; 5-ascetic; 6-vicarious; 7-rationalize; 8-obsequious; 9-sublimate; 10-wanton

---

Keep your pencil ready. This is a work book and a word game book, and we want you to write in it continually. The only way you can gain ownership of new words is by using them.

Now take the following eight words and change them into other parts of speech according to the instructions. Be as sure as you can in each case that the resulting sentence makes sense.

1. Change *vicarious* to an adverb, as, *to travel*.....................

2. Change *rationalize* to a noun, as, *You are guilty of* ....

3. Change *gregarious* to a noun, as, *No one doubts the* ....*of human beings.*

4. Change *obsequious* to an adverb, as, *He obeyed* ....

5. Change *ascetic* to a noun referring to practice, as, *The religious novice practiced* ....

6. Change *pander* to a noun, as, *He is a* .... *to the greed of others.*

7. Change *sublimate* to an adjective, as, *His* .... *passion gives power to his poetry.*

8. Change *wanton* to a noun, as, *The* .... *of the court of Charles II is proverbial.*

ANSWERS: 1-vicariously; 2-rationalization; 3-gregariousness; 4-obsequiously; 5-asceticism; 6-panderer; 7-sublimated; 8-wantonness

---

From your work so far with these ten words, you should have a fairly good idea by now of how they may be used in sentences, even if you may have met some of them for the first time. Test yourself. Without referring to the list on the previous page, try to fill in the required word in the sentences that follow. Note that any one of the several forms of each word may be needed. Better use your pencil. The mere physical act of writing a word down will help to fix it in your mind.

1. Marie is too .... to be happy without friends.

2. The waiter bowed .... to every wealthy customer who came into the restaurant.

3. His dissipated life has sapped his ambition and health and made him ....

4. The motion picture was so sickeningly .... that most of the audience left in disgust.

5. Mothers feel a .... pleasure in their children's accomplishments.

6. Be honest with yourself. Don't try to .... your bad motives.

7. He lived the life of a (an) ....; for he abhorred self-indulgence and enjoyed solitude.

8. The dishonest politician .... to the greed and thoughtlessness of the mob.

9. Some say that all great art is a .... of the primitive instincts.

10. She led a fruitless, ..., uncontrolled life.

ANSWERS: 1-gregarious; 2-obsequiously; 3-effete; 4-maudlin; 5-vicarious; 6-rationalize; 7-ascetic; 8-panders; 9-sublimation; 10-wanton

------

Remember this: Once an adult has finished his schooling, he rarely adds more than 25 new words to his vocabulary each year thereafter. Already, in one session, you have at least increased your knowledge of these ten words, even though you may have met them before. Therefore, whenever you add ten new words to your vocabulary you will have done almost as much as most people do in six months.

Be sure, though, that you *keep* these words. Can you recall all ten of them now without referring to the text? If you *can* do this, then practice spelling them and pronouncing them, out loud if possible. If there are one or two of them that are hard to remember, why not write them down and practice on them from time to time?

WORDS ABOUT DOCTORS AND SPECIALISTS

Of course you know that you have two different kinds of vocabulary, and that one is much larger than the other.

Your *recognition* vocabulary is made up of the words that you can "recognize" and understand when you read them or hear them spoken.

Your *functional* vocabulary includes the words that you can recall and use when *you yourself* speak.

Your recognition vocabulary is about three times as large as your functional vocabulary.

If, as an example, you study French and you learn merely to read that language, you will find that you will be unable to speak it because you are practiced only in recognizing the words when you see them, but not in recalling them when you don't see them.

Or, conversely, if you are taught only to speak French, you will fail when it comes to reading the language because you have not had any practice in understanding or "recognizing" the printed words.

In order to develop both types of vocabulary it is therefore important that you not only *read* the words that are new to you in this book and *write* them down, but that you say them *out loud*.

One other thing. When you talk, the words and their meanings are conveyed to others by the sound of your voice. This process of speaking, by the way, is not so simple as it seems. Every word that you say out loud uses 72 muscles in your face and throat.

Therefore, respect your voice. Be conscious of it. How does it sound to your ear? If you would care to know, try standing in a corner of your room. Read or say some words out loud. If you want a still simpler method just put your hand behind your ear and speak. Is your voice attractive to you? If it isn't, practice a bit. Relax. Use the lower tones. You will find them more musical.

Now we shall turn to a new group of words. In the last chapter we dealt with such general and abstract concepts as "rationalize," and "maudlin." In this present chapter we will consider more specific items.

The field of medicine is close to your life, so we will introduce you to a few of the doctors and specialists you may have to consult at some time.

I. The *obstetrician* delivers babies. First assistant to the stork, he practices *obstetrics* (ob-ste-trish′-an; ob-stet′-riks).

The *pediatrician* takes over when the obstetrician has finished. He specializes in the treatment of infants and very young children, and the profession he practices is called *pediatrics* (pee-dee-a-trish′-an; pee-dee-at′-riks).

The *podiatrist* treats the minor ailments of your feet (po-dye′-a-trist). He is also often called a *chiropodist* (kye-rop′-o-dist).

The *osteopath* works on the theory that diseases arise chiefly from the displacement of bones, with resultant pressure on nerve centers and blood vessels. Hence, his treatment is manipulation of the affected parts. He practices *osteopathy* (oss'-tee-o-path; oss-tee-op'-ath-ee).

The *oculist* or *ophthalmologist* is a medical doctor and often a trained surgeon who treats the troubles and the diseases of the eyes. He is not to be confused with

The *optometrist,* who is not a medical doctor. The optometrist examines the eyes for the sole purpose of prescribing spectacles or eyeglasses. Nor should either one be confused with

The *optician,* who, again, is not a doctor. This man is a merchant and manufacturer, making and selling eyeglasses, lenses, binoculars (ok'-you-list; off-thal-mol'-o-jist; op-tom'-e-trist; op-tish'-an).

The *gynecologist* specializes in the diseases that are peculiar to women (jyne-e-kol'-o-jist).

The *dermatologist* is a skin-man. When you have a rash, acne, certain allergies, skin lesions, psoriasis, or any skin affection, he's the man to see (der-ma-tol'-o-jist).

The *psychiatrist* is a graduate medical doctor who concerns himself with mental aberrations and with the various psychoses that afflict the mind (sye-kye'-a-trist).

The *orthodontist* neither fills nor extracts teeth. He specializes in straightening crooked teeth, and in correcting bad "bites," or, as they are called in the vocabulary of *orthodontia,* "malocclusions" (orth-o-don'-tist; orth-o-don'-sha).

II. *Which specialist would you call in?* Now you had better review the words you have just had, as we are going to give you a checkup to see if they are fixed in your mind. Pick up your pencil and write down the title of the specialist you would suggest for each of the following ailments. This is a test of your functional vocabulary.

1. You have a painful corn, ...

2. You need to know what type of eyeglasses are best suited to you, ...

3. Your baby has the colic, ...

4. You need a doctor to deliver your baby, ...

5. A friend of yours has had a complete mental collapse, ...

6. A child you know has a badly formed jaw, ...

7. A woman is suffering from female disorders, ...

8. You are troubled with a skin rash, ...

9. You have an eye disease that needs expert attention, ...

10. You have an illness which you believe can be cured by bone manipulation, ...

11. You want to buy a new pair of glasses, ...

ANSWERS: 1-podiatrist or chiropodist; 2-optometrist; 3-pediatrician; 4-obstetrician; 5-psychiatrist; 6-orthodontist; 7-gynecologist; 8-dermatologist; 9-oculist or ophthalmologist; 10-osteopath; 11-optician

---

III. *Test your ingenuity:* We have discussed a number of doctors and in a few instances we have mentioned the names of their specialties. Below you will find a list of specialists. Write in the blank space opposite each one the name of his type of work. For example, a doctor practices *medicine,* a dentist *dentistry.* Use your memory where possible, your common sense in other cases. The answers below will tell you how successful you are at seeing logical relationships between parts of speech.

The Doctor	His Work
1. obstetrician	....
2. pediatrician	....
3. podiatrist	....
4. chiropodist	....
5. osteopath	....
6. oculist or ophthalmologist	....
7. optometrist	....
8. gynecologist	....
9. dermatologist	....
10. psychiatrist	....
11. orthodontist	....

ANSWERS: 1-obstetrics; 2-pediatrics; 3-podiatry; 4-chiropody; 5-osteopathy; 6-ophthalmology; 7-optometry; 8-gynecology; 9-dermatology; 10-psychiatry; 11-orthodontia

———————

IV. *Is there a doctor in the house?* The terms in this chapter and the specialties they involve will be particularly hard for you to remember unless you have been previously familiar with them. It may pay to close these exercises with one more game in order that these words may be photographed on your mind.

If you find yourself tired, skip this until tomorrow. And yet the present topic may be so familiar to you that the tests will prove very easy.

You are taking a tour of the Professional Building in some large city. You are going to see a number of medical titles on the doors as you go down the halls.

In each case check the one definition or description that you believe to be correct. Either a, b or c. Before you look at the answers see if you can identify or name the professions of the two out of three that are left.

This is a combination functional and recognition vocabulary test:

Room One: The shingle says: "John Doe, *Podiatrist.*"

  a. He treats diseases of the skin.

  b. He's the man to see when you have an aching corn.

  c. He practices general medicine.

Room Two: The office of Richard Roe, *Psychiatrist.*

  a. He treats diseases of the skin.

  b. He corrects malocclusions of the teeth.

  c. People who have mental aberrations are taken to him.

Room Three: The office of that eminent George Jones, *Oculist* or *Ophthalmologist.*

  a. He knows all about diseases of the eye and refractive errors, and often resorts to surgery to correct the eye ailments of his patients.

b. He'll examine your eyes and write out for you a prescription for glasses.

c. He'll be happy to sell you any sort of optical instruments—specs, binoculars, telescopes, microscopes.

Room Four: The office of James Brown, *Osteopath*. If you believe in drugless therapy, you'll be interested in visiting him.

a. His specialty is bunions.

b. Holding that diseases arise chiefly from displacement of the bones, with resultant pressure on nerves and blood vessels, he remedies the evil by manipulation of the affected parts.

c. He fills and extracts teeth.

Room Five: The name on this door is John Smith, *Obstetrician*.

a. He treats diseases peculiar to women.

b. He specializes in the ills of infancy and childhood.

c. He delivers babies.

ANSWERS: 1-b, (a) is a dermatologist, (c) a doctor, physician or general practitioner; 2-c, (a) is a dermatologist; (b) an orthodontist; 3-a, (b) is an optometrist; (c) an optician; 4-b, (a) is a podiatrist or chiropodist; (c) a dentist; 5-c, (a) is a gynecologist; (b) a pediatrician

You have finished what is, perhaps, a somewhat difficult chapter. Medical terms, on the whole, are artificial words that have not come into being in a natural way, but have been invented by man to identify new specialties as they appeared. For this reason these words may be especially hard to recall.

The more familiar you become with them, however, the more easily you will be able to recognize and remember other words in the field of medicine and so add them to your growing vocabulary.

Always bear in mind that each new word you acquire will open up new vistas to your mind and will have a subtle and beneficial influence on your life.

VERBS GIVE YOU POWER

Do you remember your old schoolbook definition of a verb? It went something like this:

"A verb is that part of speech which asserts, declares or predicates something."

But a dynamic verb is more than this. It is the catalyst of the sentence. That is, it is the word that brings the sentence to life.

Choose your verbs with care.

If you pick a dull verb, your speech will be dull, barely serving its primary purpose of communication. It will be merely a succession of syllables that will make little impression on the mind of your reader or listener.

A choice of powerful verbs, on the other hand, will make your speech electric, galvanic. Like a powder charge, it can give the impact of bullets to all the other words in your sentence.

A single illustration of this statement will be enough. Which of the two following sentences has the greater force?

1. He is a moral leper; let us keep away from him and have nothing to do with him.

2. He is a moral leper; let us *ostracize* him.

45

The answer is obvious, isn't it? One word has expressed the meaning of ten.

So watch your verbs. They are packed with power.

I. Here are ten dynamic verbs that belong in a rich vocabulary. We are not going to give you their precise definitions. Just read the sentences in which they occur and see if you can guess the meanings of the ones you don't already know. Pronounce them aloud.

What are some of the things people do?

1. They *expiate* (ex'-pee-ate) their sins, crimes, blunders, or errors.

2. They *importune* (im-por-tyoon') God for divine favors.

3. They *impute* (im-pyoot') unworthy motives to their enemies.

4. They *scintillate* (sin'-til-late), the wittier ones, at gay gatherings.

5. They *mulct* (mulkt) the unwary or gullible public.

6. They *ostracize* (oss'-tra-size) members of religious, political, or racial minorities.

7. They *deprecate* (dep'-re-kate) the sins of this age.

8. They *procrastinate* (pro-krass'-ti-nate) and then vow to be more punctual in the future.

9. They *rusticate* (russ'-ti-kate) in the summer time, if finances permit.

10. They *vegetate* (vej'-e-tate) all year, if they are lacking in imagination, initiative or energy.

II. Referring to Section I only where necessary, write the proper verb next to its definition. The definitions do not appear in the same order as the sentences above.

1. Live in a passive way ....

2. Deprive of a possession unjustly ....

3. Make amends for ....

4. Beg for ceaselessly; beseech; entreat ....

5. Exclude from public or private favor; to ban ....

6. Put off until a future time; delay ....

7. Sparkle with wit or humor ....

8. Spend time in the country ....

9. To ascribe, attribute, charge an act or thought to someone, usually in a bad or accusatory sense ....

10. Disapprove of the actions of some- one ....

ANSWERS: 1-vegetate; 2-mulct; 3-expiate; 4-importune; 5-ostra- cize; 6-procrastinate; 7-scintillate; 8-rusticate; 9-im- pute; 10-deprecate.

III. Which of the verbs you have just had would most aptly describe the characteristic action of each of the following people?

1. He is too indolent to get his work
done on time. He.....................

2. He is accustomed to blaming others. He.....................

3. He is a gay and witty person. He.....................

4. He possesses a lively conscience. He.....................

5. He is a person who is in a rut and
leading a lazy life. He.....................

6. He is an exclusive individual. He.....................

7. He doesn't mind cheating others. He.....................

8. He's an insistent beggar. He.....................

9. He is ashamed of the acts of his as-
sociates. He.....................

10. He is on a vacation at a farmhouse. He.....................

ANSWERS: 1-procrastinates; 2-imputes; 3-scintillates; 4-expiates;
5-vegetates; 6-ostracizes; 7-mulcts; 8-importunes;
9-deprecates; 10-rusticates

———————

IV. In each of the following divisions you will find two sentences. The first sentence has a group of italicized words. The second sentence has a blank space. In each case a slightly different form of one of the verbs you have just studied can be substituted for the group of italicized words before it. Decide what this form is, and write it in.

1. He has been *spending his time in the country*. He has been...........................

2. Why do you keep *nagging me for favors?* Why are you so ....?

3. He took $1,000,000 from the public *by dishonest methods*. He .... the public of $1,000,000.

4. *Excluding him from our group* is our most potent weapon against the liar. .... is our most potent weapon against the liar.

5. For the past two years, I have been *accomplishing nothing and getting nowhere*. For the past two years, I have been ....

6. He *pled against* the exploitation of labor. He .... the exploitation of labor.

7. In *atonement for* his sin, he did penance for three days. In .... of his sin, he did penance for three days.

8. Do they *accuse* me *of committing these offenses?* Have they .... these offenses to me?

9. I resent your *accusation that I committed* these offenses. I resent your .... of these offenses to me.

10. She is a *gay and witty* speaker. She is a .... speaker.

11. *Putting off till tomorrow* is the thief of time................ is the thief of time.

ANSWERS: 1-rusticating; 2-importunate; 3-mulcted; 4-ostracism; 5-vegetating; 6-deprecated; 7-expiation; 8-imputed; 9-imputation; 10-scintillating; 11-procrastination

V. Now for a change of pace, with a few verbal gymnastics for you. Can you think of five verbs ending in *ate*? They have not appeared in this chapter. The definitions and initial letters are offered to help you.

1. Have control over   D ....

2. Make easier   F ....

3. Follow the example of   E ....

4. Make gestures of motions as in
   speaking   G ....

5. Get better   R ....

ANSWERS: 1-dominate (dom'-i-nate); 2-facilitate (fa-sil'-i-tate); 3-emulate (em'-you-late); 4-gesticulate (jess-tik'-you-late); 5-recuperate (ree-kyoo'-per-ate)

———————

Now can you think of five verbs ending in *ize?*

1. Exercise condescension toward   P ....

2. Make pay a fine, or suffer punishment P ....

3. Make vivid or moving   D ....

4. Make live forever   I ....

5. Appropriate and give out as one's own
   the literary work of another   P ....

ANSWERS: 1-patronize (pate'-run-ize); 2-penalize (pee'-nal-ize); 3-dramatize (dram'-a-tize); 4-immortalize (im-mor'-tal-ize); 5-plagiarize (play'-jee-a-rize)

VI. Can you make the verbs of Section V an active part of your speaking vocabulary? Fill the blanks of the following sentences. Some new form of the verb may be required, such as *dominates, dominating, dominated*.

1. Beethoven has always .... the musical scene.

2. Carl Sandburg's biography vividly .... the life of Lincoln as no other book has ever been able to.

3. I have never seen a sick man .... so quickly.

4. Your friends think you are stuck up because you seem to .... them.

5. Nature will .... you for your alcoholic excesses.

6. Let us .... the habits of successful men.

7. In her confusion, she .... wildly.

8. He built an insecure and dishonest literary reputation by .... the classics.

9. Let me pack for you; that will .... your departure.

10. The "Elegy in a Country Churchyard" did much to .... the poet, Thomas Gray.

ANSWERS: 1-dominated; 2-dramatizes; 3-recuperate; 4-patronize; 5-penalize; 6-emulate; 7-gesticulated; 8-plagiarizing; 9-facilitate; 10-immortalize

———————

VII. Twenty dynamic verbs, excellent additions to a powerful vocabulary, have been discussed in this chapter.

How many of them can you call back to your mind? Try and see, but, of course, don't refer to the preceding pages until you have to give up.

In order to help your memory, the initial letters are given. Recall and write down as many as you can. Ten will be fair, fifteen extremely good.

E	....	D	....
I	....	F	....
I	....	E	....
S	....	G	....
M	....	R	....
O	....	P	....
D	....	P	....
P	....	D	....
R	....	I	....
V	....	P	....

For the next few days keep your eyes and ears alert for verbs. Note them as you read, or as people speak to you. See whether they are effective and do their work. Even billboards, car-cards and other advertisements will help you. Advertising space costs money and the publicity men have to pick their verbs with care. See if you can improve on the experts. How many synonyms can you find for the verbs they use? Are your choices better or worse? As you read your newspaper, watch for examples of verbs.

Here are a few samples from our best speakers:

"Mr. Sherwood has given us a drama which *stimulates* the thought processes."—GLADYS SWARTHOUT.

"We have followed the President's leadership in his efforts to *revitalize* our democracy."—HAROLD L. ICKES.

"In the face of terrific problems we cannot *pursue* our customary life."—CORDELL HULL.

So take care of your verbs. They will add power to your speech.

WORDS ABOUT THEORIES

Intelligent dinner-table conversation will help to give your new words a good tryout. But when you invite people in for dinner do you always limit your party to your old friends and neighbors? We are all apt to do this, simply because we tend to be lazy. There is little conversational challenge, however, to old friends. Everyone puts on a pair of comfortable slippers and settles down to an evening of gossip. If, however, you mix a new couple with the old crowd, watch how your friends will get on their toes then and try to sell themselves! You will find this tremendously stimulating and the conversation will begin to sparkle.

At such a time the table-talk may easily swing to politics, or to personal theories on philosophy and religion. Here we come into one of those higher uses of thought that make severe demands on our knowledge of English. The mentally alert person is not content to live merely from day to day, completely circumscribed by such things as food, money, clothing and entertainment. Occasionally he is tempted to speculate on *why* he is living and on what the controlling forces of his life are. This chapter deals with a few of the names or word symbols that are applied to these motivating forces by different people who have varying points of view.

1. Is there a God? Nothing so closely approaches the outer limits of abstraction as theorizing about a supernatural and supreme being. Many of us worship, most of us at least accept, some form of deity. Do you belong to the minority who insist, often belligerently, that man makes God in his own image, that God is a figment of the imagination and hence completely, irrevocably non-existent? Then you are an *atheist* (ay'-thee-ist, *th* as in *think*) and your philosophy is called *atheism* (ay'-thee-izm). The word is from the Greek *a*, "without" and *theos*, "god."

2. To many other thinkers it seems more reasonable to say that the existence or non-existence of a supreme being is one mystery the human mind will never fathom. How did the world come into being? How did life begin? Is there a Father who looks after his children, or are we the products of purposeless chance? Do you answer these questions by saying that no one knows and no one can ever hope to know? Then you are an *agnostic* (ag-noss'-tik) and your doctrine is called *agnosticism* (ag-noss'-ti-sizm). Again this is from the Greek *agnostos* which means "not knowing."

3. Why did that young child dart across the roadway just as a huge truck rounded the bend? How do you explain the needless snuffing out of an innocent life? Is it due to blind chance? To cause and effect? Why should some great benefactor of humanity be cut off in his prime? Are such events controlled by accident? By fate? This word *fate* is derived from the Latin *fatus*, which means "spoken" or "predicted."

Do you believe that everything that happens is predetermined, foreordained, written down, as it were, on the far-off pages of some mighty volume? Then you are a *fatalist* (fay'tal-ist) and your theory is called *fatalism* (fay'tal-izm).

4. In this world of ours you will find many people who think only of themselves and of their own selfish advantage, and who actually believe that all virtue consists in the pursuit of self-interest. They make this their religion. Do you think continually of yourself? Are you completely indifferent to the feelings and wishes of others? You are an *egoist* (egg'-o-ist) and your creed is called *egoism* (egg' o-izm). Characteristically this word is from the Latin *ego* meaning "I."

5. If, however, your characteristics are opposite to those of an egoist, and if you have an unselfish regard for and devotion to the interests of others, you are an *altruist* (al'-troo-ist) and you practice *altruism* (al'-troo-izm). The relationship of this word to the Latin *alter* meaning "other" is plainly understandable.

6. Can you rise above petty considerations of pleasure and pain, joy and grief? Can you meet adversity with indifference, and submit to the arrows and slings of misfortune with a dignified resignation? Can you put away envy, greed, jealousy and hatred and the appetites and passions of the world? Can you suffer mental and physical pain without complaint? If you can honestly do such things as these and if you sincerely believe that this is the better scheme of living you will be named a *stoic* (sto'-ik) and are a practitioner of *stoicism,* (sto'-i-sizm). The founder of stoicism was the Greek philosopher Zeno who lived about 300 years before Christ. "Stoic" is from the Greek

word *stoikos,* which, in turn, is from *stoa,* meaning "porch." Zeno taught in the *Stoa Poikile* or "Painted Porch" situated in Athens.

7. Are you apt to say: "No other nation can hold a candle to my country. We are the supermen, the chosen people. Every other race is inferior to mine and they are all destined to be our slaves when the day comes"? This is not patriotism. Or, rather, it is patriotism carried to an illogical and ludicrous extreme. Do you happen to talk this way? Then you are a *chauvinist* (sho'-vin-ist) and you are a follower of *chauvinism* (sho'-vin-izm). This word is based on the name of a real man, Nicolas Chauvin of Rochefort, who was so demonstrative in his devotion to Napoleon and the imperial cause that he was ridiculed on the French stage at the time.

8. Are you a braggart about your country's power? Do you always want your nation to use force? Do you want to call out the fleet, the air armada and the army, on the slightest provocation, and send our soldiers and sailors round the world to show those "damn foreigners" who's the boss? Do the other nations want war? We'll give it to them. And if they don't want it we'll give it to them anyway. If this should be a description of your philosophy, then you are a *jingoist* (jing'-go-ist) and your heart beats in tune with the martial music of *jingoism* (jing'-go-izm). The "Jingoes" were originally a section of the Conservative party in England in 1877 who were eager to have their nation support the Turks in the Russo-Turkish war.

9. Is it best that our government should follow the political faith, methods and tenets of our fathers and grand-

fathers, or shall we move rapidly ahead, change constantly, explore and experiment? Those who believe in *liberalism* follow the latter philosophy. They owe allegiance to no party, are independent in thought and action and are always anathema to those who wish the government to pursue the well-trod paths. *Liberals* prefer a changing, dynamic, experimenting government. They vote for progress, sometimes in the sense that anything new and different and previously untried is progressive. The Romans gave us the word *liber,* meaning "free."

10. The *conservative,* on the other hand, is opposed to change. He believes that what is, is best. He prefers that his government follow the familiar, tried, tested, safe, and supposedly sane, policies. "We're content with what we have. Why take the risk of sailing into uncharted waters?" Here we can go back again to the Latin, this time to *conservare* meaning "to preserve."

Liberalism is dynamic. *Conservatism* is static. In politics these two wings of the government are to the left and right, respectively. Extreme liberals, still further to the left, are called *radicals.* Extreme conservatives, who are far to the right, are called *reactionaries.* Conservatives want to keep things as they are. Reactionaries wish to turn the clock back to "the good old days." "Radical" is from the Latin *radicalis* meaning "pertaining to roots" or "thoroughgoing" and "reactionary" goes back to the Latin *re* (back) and *agere* (to lead).

11. What type of life is the best? To one group of thinkers that question has a simple answer. That life is the most successful, says the *epicurean* (ep-i-kyoo-ree´-an),

which brings to each person the maximum of pleasure and the minimum of pain. The doctrine of *epicureanism* (ep-i-kyoo-ree'-an-izm) teaches that pleasure is the chief good. In these modern days the meaning of the word has changed somewhat, and an epicurean is thought of more particularly as one who enjoys the delights of the table and who is expert and fastidious in his choice of food. This philosophy was founded by Epicurus, the Greek scholar who lived about three centuries before Christ.

At this point you had better review the words that you have studied in this chapter. You are going to be asked some questions about them.

Which one of the people whose philosophies have been described in the preceding paragraphs would be most apt to make each of the following statements?

1. "I'm interested in the welfare of the other fellow, not in my own." ....

2. "Let the other fellow take care of himself. My interests come first, last and always." ....

3. "My nation is the only one in the world that has any good points." ....

4. "Let's not stand still in politics. Progress, change, experimentation,—that's what we need!" ....

5. "Happiness, pleasure, fun, good eating: these are the most important things in life." ....

6. "There's a God? Don't be silly. Only stupid people believe in God." ....

7. "Maybe there is a God. Maybe there isn't. I don't know, and I don't believe anybody else does or ever will know."   ....

8. "The wise and brave man is indifferent to pain and pleasure."   ....

9. "We'll build up our troops and our navy, we'll arm to the hilt. Then we'll dare any nation in the world to knock the chip off our shoulder!"   ....

10. "You can't change the future. It's all planned and written down."   ....

11. "Let's keep things just as they are. We're getting along all right, so why fool around with any dangerous, half-baked, new-fangled theories."   ....

ANSWERS: 1-altruist; 2-egoist; 3-chauvinist; 4-liberal or radical; 5-epicurean; 6-atheist; 7-agnostic; 8-stoic; 9-jingoist; 10-fatalist; 11-conservative or reactionary

---

Adjectives can, of course, be made of all the nouns that have appeared in this chapter. Here are the forms that they take.

1. altruism—altruistic
2. atheism—atheistic
3. agnosticism—agnostic
4. fatalism—fatalistic
5. egoism—egoistic
6. stoicism—stoical
7. chauvinism—chauvinistic
8. jingoism—jingoistic
9. liberalism—liberal
10. conservatism—conservative
11. epicureanism—epicurean

Now, referring to the preceding list, try to fit the correct adjective into each of the following phrases.

1. The .... attitude of the ungodly.

2. The .... doubts of the skeptical.

3. Age tends to bring a .... tinge to one's politics.

4. Politically, youth is inclined to be ....

5. The .... flavor of oriental religions.

6. The narrow .... desires of the conceited.

7. The .... resignation of those who have suffered much.

8. The .... blatancy of professional "flag-wavers."

9. The .... desires of the self-indulgent.

10. The .... diplomacy of the munitions-makers.

11. The .... work of Marie and Pierre Curie.

ANSWERS: 1-atheistic;   2-agnostic;   3-conservative;   4-liberal;
5-fatalistic; 6-egoistic; 7-stoical; 8-chauvinistic; 9-epicurean; 10-jingoistic; 11-altruistic

---

Unless you have met these words before you will find their definitions hard to keep in mind. But they are words of power, and a powerful vocabulary is one that can put into effective words the thoughts and feelings you have in your mind. More than that, new words will actually give you *new* and *deeper* thoughts and feelings and will strengthen and enrich your thinking.

QUICK VOCABULARY BUILDER

Our English speech is a reservoir of the classical languages. It has taken over to itself and has absorbed for its own use more than one quarter of the entire Greek language and more than fifty per cent of the entire Latin language. It is obvious, then, that a knowledge of Greek and Latin stems is invaluable in any program of vocabulary building.

In the exercises ahead we will take English words apart and will show how you can easily identify and define hundreds of words that you may never have seen before.

I. The Greek stem *gamos,* which literally means "marriage," usually appears as an ending in English in the form *gamy.* This has given rise to a large word family.

(1) *Monogamy* (mon-og′-a-mee): The Americans practice monogamy and are a monogamous (mon-og′-a-muss) race. This, of course, means a system of marriage where a husband has only one wife. The term comes from two Greek words: *monos,* "one" and *gamos,* "marriage."

(2) *Bigamy* (big′-a-mee): A "bigamist," as you remember, is a man with two wives. Here we have a combination of two languages: *bi* means "two" in

Latin, and combined with *gamos* we therefore have "two marriages."

(3) *Polygamy* (po-lig'-a-mee): This means several wives to one husband, as formerly practiced by the Mormons in Utah. Such married people were *polygamists* (po-lig'-a-mists). *Poly* in Greek means "many."

(4) *Misogamy* (miss-og'-a-mee): This term means hatred of marriage and a person who holds this view is known as a *misogamist* (miss-og'-a-mist). *Misos,* when translated from the Greek, means "hatred."

II. Now notice how the above Greek and Latin stems will branch out and lead to still more new words.

(1) *Monotheism* (mon'-o-thee-izm, *th* as in *think*): This is the philosophy of the *monotheist* who believes in one god: Greek *monos* combined with *theos* signifying "god."

(2) *Bicuspid* (bye-cuss'-pid): A tooth with two prongs on the lower end of it. You have already learned the translation of *bi; cuspid* is from the Latin *cuspis* meaning "point."

(3) *Polyglot* (pol'-ee-glot): *Glotta* is Greek for "tongue" or "language." So the polyglot is one who speaks many tongues or many languages.

(4) *Misanthropy* (miss-an'-thro-pee): *Anthropos* in Greek means "man." We have, then, the hatred of man or of mankind. A *misanthrope* (miss'-anthrope), therefore, is anyone who has a morbid aversion to, or distrust of, his fellow men.

III. Still more discoveries can be made with the roots that you have learned.

(1) *Theology* (thee-ol′-o-jee, *th* as in *think*) is the knowledge of God and religion. To *theos* we add the Greek ending *-logia* which means "knowledge." The usual way that *-logia* appears in English words is in the form of "logy."

(2) *Philanthropy* (fil-an′-thro-pee) is the direct opposite of misanthropy. Philanthropy means the love of mankind; the root *anthropos* which you already know is combined with the Greek word *philos* meaning "love of." A philanthropist, then, who gives money to the poor, is literally a "lover of his fellow men."

IV. Now, if we are to combine the two new stems in the above section, we have:

(1) *Anthropology* (an-thro-pol′-o-jee), which you can now interpret as the "knowledge of man" or the history of the human race, and

(2) *Philology* (fil-ol′-o-jee), which should mean "love of knowledge," which is what it did mean in Greek. Later it came to mean more especially the love of words and the study of language, and is usually used today in that sense.

You now have an ownership in nine important Greek or Latin stems, which, in their usual English forms, are:

mono —one	theo	—god
bi —two	anthropo —man	
poly —many	philo	—love of
miso —hatred of	logy	—knowledge, study of
gamy —marriage		

V. Can you qualify as a good detective? Keep in mind the nine stems we have just discussed and try to arrive at the meanings of the following words. Guess intelligently, and only refer back to the roots if you have to. Write your meaning in the blank.

1. Many Englishmen wear MONocles (mon'-o-kulz).

   ....

2. He delivered an interesting MONOlogue (mon'-o-log).

   ....

3. He has a MONOpoly of the trade (mo-nop'-o-lee).

   ....

4. He lives in a MONastery (mon'-ass-tair-ee).

   ....

5. He is riding a BIcycle (bye'-sickle).   ....

6. Man is a BIped (bye'-ped).   ....

7. France and England made a BIlateral (bye-lat'-er-al) agreement.

   ....

8. A rectangle is a POLYgon (pol'-ee-gon).

   ....

9. A MISOgynist (miss-oj'-i-nist) shuns the company of women.

   ....

10. Romans practiced POLYtheism (pol'-ee-thee'-izm, *th* as in *think*).

   ....

11. The apoTHEOsis (ap-o-thee'-o-sis, *th* as in *think*) of Hitler by the German people. ....

12. President Roosevelt's stamp collection was the envy of PHILatelists (fi-lat'-el-ists). ....

13. The ANTHROPOid (an'-thro-poyd) apes are similar in appearance to humans. ....

14. BioLOGY (bye-ol'-o-jee) is a fascinating science. ....

15. England is a MONarchy (mon'-ark-ee). ....

ANSWERS: 1-lens for ONE eye; 2-speech by ONE person; 3-control by ONE person of the market; 4-place where people live ALONE; 5-vehicle of TWO wheels; 6-creature with TWO feet; 7-TWO-sided; 8-MANY-sided figure; 9-HATER of women; 10-belief in MANY gods; 11-raising to GODhood; 12-LOVERS, hence collectors, of stamps; 13-MANlike; 14-STUDY of life; 15-country where ONE person rules

---

VI. It will be good practice for you, if you will, to check over and pronounce *out loud* the words you have learned:

1. GAMY—marriage	2. MONO—one	3. BI—two
monogamy	monotheism	bigamy
bigamy	monogamy	bicuspid
polygamy	monocle	bicycle
misogamy	monologue	biped
	monopoly	bilateral
	monastery	
	monarchy	

4. POLY—many
polygamy
polyglot
polygon
polytheism

5. MISO—hatred of
misogamy
misogynist
misanthropy

6. THEO—god
theology
monotheism
apotheosis

7. ANTHROPO
—man
misanthropy
anthropoid
anthropology
philanthropy

8. PHILO—
love of
philology
philatelist
philanthropy

9. LOGY—
knowledge,
study of
biology
theology
philology
anthropology

We believe that the scientific method used in this chapter of breaking up words into their component parts and then tracing them to their roots, will show you a quick and simple way to learn many new words.

The object of this book, you see, is not merely to help you enlarge your vocabulary, but to offer you various practical hints that will make it easier for you to go on with this work long after you have finished the last page.

TEST YOUR PROGRESS

You are of course aware that you will never add importantly to your vocabulary by merely being *exposed* to words; or by reading; or by talking. *You must have a plan*.

Here is one way to get ahead with words in everyday life. It's the simplest thing in the world.

Buy a small pocket notebook. When you read the papers, a magazine, or a book, or listen to the radio, and come upon a strange word, check it. Then look it up in the dictionary. If you find that it's some abstruse or highly technical term, such as, say, *syzygy*, "an immovable union between two brachials of a crinoid," just pass it by. You won't be using it unless you are studying to be a professor of biology. But if it sounds like a word that will be helpful to you, enter it in your notebook, together with its pronunciation and its most common meaning. Be sure, also, to copy from the dictionary the sample sentence in which it is used, if such an example is given.

All this will take only a minute or so, but it is necessary to make the practice a daily habit. Then the list in your notebook will grow and grow, as will your command of English speech.

We want, at this point, to help you gain complete possession of any of the words in the first eight chapters that may have been unfamiliar to you.

In this review of what has gone before you have the privilege of marking yourself! After you have compared your answers with those given at the end of the text, and have graded your own paper, we will give you an interpretation of your score and you can then see what progress you have made.

I. 1. The study of the origins of words or of word histories is called:

a-philology; b-verbology; c-etymology (2 points credit).

2. The "taxicabs" in Ancient Rome gave rise to our word:

a-calculate; b-supercilious; c-captain (2 points credit).

3. The Greek syllable *graph* means: a-seeing; b-writing; c-speaking (2 points credit).

4. The word *run* has approximately .... different dictionary meanings: a-3; b-20; c-90 (2 points credit).

5. Some words require emotional maturity so they may be understood: Is the statement a-true; b-false (2 points credit).

II. Each phrase in column B applies to one particular word in column A (2 points credit for each correct answer).

A	B
1. vicarious	a. Appeal to the baser emotions
2. rationalize	b. Tearfully sentimental
3. gregarious	c. Company-loving
4. obsequious	d. Second-hand or substituted experience
5. maudlin	e. Fawning and servile
6. ascetic	f. Justify a not too worthy act
7. pander	g. Severely self-denying
8. sublimate	h. Refine; purify; turn into higher channels
9. wanton	i. Worn out; sterile; barren
10. effete	j. Unrestrained

III. Check the correct forms (2 points credit for each correct answer).

1. The obstetrician: a-delivers babies; b-treats babies; c-treats women's diseases.

2. The osteopath: a-straightens teeth; b-specializes in skin diseases; c-treats diseases by manipulating the bones.

3. The optometrist: a-sells lenses; b-measures your eyes for glasses; c-operates on your eyes.

4. The podiatrist: a-treats foot ailments; b-treats mental ailments; c-treats nerve ailments.

5. The psychiatrist is interested in: a-your stomach; b-your mind; c-your eyes.

IV. Write the required verb (2 points credit for each correct answer).

1. To stagnate   V ....
2. To postpone   P ....
3. To cheat; to fine unjustly   M ....
4. To exclude; to ban   O ....
5. To atone for   E ....
6. To entreat   I ....
7. To sparkle   S ....
8. To disapprove   D ....
9. To spend time in the country R ....
10. To charge someone with   I ....

V. Take sentence #1 below. Would a chauvinist have said this? If so, write "chauvinist" in the blank space. Fill in each blank space with the type of person who would be most apt to have said the particular sentence (2 points for each correct answer).

1. "I have good taste in foods and wines." ....
2. "Government should experiment."   ....
3. "Government must not experiment."   ....
4. "If they don't want war, give it to them anyway."

                                          ....
5. "My country is the only one worth anything."

                                          ....

6. "Pain will never make me wince."   ....

7. "The other fellow comes first."   ....

8. "I come first above all."   ....

9. "There is no God."   ....

10. "I don't know whether or not there is a God."

....

11. "Everything will happen as it will, no matter what we do."   ....

VI. Give the meaning of each of the following Greek elements—here given in their usual English combining forms (2 points credit for each correct answer).

1. logy	2. philo	3. anthropo
4. theo	5. miso	6. poly
7. bi	8. mono	9. gamy

ANSWERS: I: 1-c; 2-a; 3-b; 4-c; 5-a

II: 1-d; 2-f; 3-c; 4-e; 5-b; 6-g; 7-a; 8-h; 9-j; 10-i

III: 1-a; 2-c; 3-b; 4-a; 5-b

IV: 1-vegetate; 2-procrastinate; 3-mulct; 4-ostracize; 5-expiate; 6-importune; 7-scintillate; 8-deprecate; 9-rusticate; 10-impute

V: 1-epicurean; 2-liberal; 3-conservative; 4-jingoist; 5-chauvinist; 6-stoic; 7-altruist; 8-egoist; 9-atheist; 10-agnostic; 11-fatalist

VI: 1-knowledge, study of; 2-love of; 3-man; 4-god; 5-hatred of; 6-many; 7-two; 8-one; 9-marriage

Sixty per cent will represent a fair mark in this review; seventy-five per cent or better will indicate a more than average ability; eighty-five per cent and up will show really excellent progress and indicates an unusual aptitude for words; forty per cent or under suggests the possibility that you may not be thorough enough as you go along.

You will find it helpful to rehearse the new words mentally for a few moments while you are walking along the street or before you go to sleep at night or during one of the many brief intervals that occur in the busiest day. Sufficient repetition and use will fix these terms in your mind for life.

WORDS ABOUT YOUR FELLOW MEN

We have now a wide and most important group of words to consider. These are the words that describe and catalog a few of the various classes of our fellow men and that identify some of their activities. And here is a helpful game that you might like to try. Just jot down on the margin of these pages, opposite each of the 25 words that follow, the name of a friend of yours or a well-known actor or public character who, you believe, would best personify the particular word under discussion. Dramatizing the word in this fashion will help fix the meaning in your mind.

You will meet some familiar words in this list, words that we have introduced in previous chapters. But repetition is a part of learning, and very often, when a word appears a second time, it will be presented under another guise and with a slightly different meaning.

Let us look over a few of the words that characterize the varied types of personalities who inhabit our interesting world.

I. 1. The *coquette* (co-ket′)—This girl promises much, flirts egregiously and delivers very little.

   2. The *circe* (sur′-see)—Her greatest pleasure comes from luring men on to their destruction.

3. The *amazon* (am'-a-zon)—She's the tall, strapping, masculine kind.

4. The *virago* (vi-ray'-go)—She is the loud-mouthed, turbulent, battle-axe type.

5. The *adonis* (a-doe'-nis)—He's the handsome, Greek-god man who makes the hearts of young girls flutter.

II. 1. The *judas* (joo'-dus)—Don't trust him. He's the traitor who will sell out his best friend for money.

2. The *futilitarian* (fyoo-til-i-tair'-ee-an)—The pessimist and cynic who sees no particular point to anything in life.

3. The *vulgarian* (vul-gair'-ee-an)—Has vulgar tastes and manners. Often used of a newly-rich person with such tastes.

4. The *pedant* (ped'-ant)—His greatest delight is making an unnecessary show of his learning. He attaches exaggerated importance to details of scholarship.

5. The *egoist* (egg'-o-ist)—His credo is selfishness. His interests come first, and no one else matters.

6. The *ascetic* (a-set'-ik)—Lives a severely temperate life and avoids the human pleasures and the human vices.

7. The *esthete* (ess'-theet, *th* as in *think*)—A person of fine taste and artistic culture. Sometimes with a little leaning to the dilettante side.

III. 1. The *demagogue* (dem'-a-gog)—He foments social discontent in order to further his own political ambitions. Huey Long, late boss of Louisiana, was the perfect example.

2. The *martinet* (mar-ti-net')—He's a fanatic in his insistence on blind discipline from his subordinates, and he's a tiresome stickler for form and etiquette.

3. The *sycophant* (sick'-o-fant)—By insincere flattery and pretended servility, he hopes to make rich or influential people think of him kindly.

IV. 1. The *atheist* (ay'-thee-ist)—He's sure God is nonexistent.

2. The *agnostic* (ag-noss'-tik)—He maintains that the human mind is incapable of penetrating the mystery of divine existence. Perhaps there is a God, perhaps not. No man knows.

V. 1. The *tyro* (tye'-ro)—He's a beginner in some trade or occupation.

2. The *virtuoso* (vur-choo-o'-so)—He is the antithesis of the tyro, having reached the greatest heights of skill and competence in music, painting or any one of the fine arts.

3. The *philologist* (fil-ol'-o-jist)—He's a scholar on the subject of language and speech.

4. The *clairvoyant* (clair-voy'-ant)—He claims the ability to see things not visible to those with normal sight. Hence, he often makes prophecies about the future.

VI. 1. The *philatelist* (fil-at'-el-ist)—He's the stamp-collector.

 2. The *numismatist* (nyoo-miss'-ma-tist)—He's the coin-collector.

VII. 1. The *gourmet* (goor-may')—Choice and dainty about his food. He has dedicated his life to good eating.

 2. The *connoisseur* (con-a-sur')—He is a critical judge of some one fine art.

VIII. Now we are going to describe each of the above types in a sentence. Can you fill in the blank space with the name of the particular type that fits the description?

1. He does not believe in God. ....

2. He is a skillful practitioner of some art. ....

3. He collects rare coins. ....

4. He has an unusual appreciation of beauty. ....

5. He is ostentatious about his learning. ....

6. He will betray a friend. ....

7. She is a flirt. ....

8. She is a destructive siren. ....

9. He is an offensive stickler for discipline. ....

10. He lives only for himself. ....

11. He lives a simple and austere existence.   ....

12. He bootlicks the rich and powerful.   ....

13. He is a false leader of the common people.   ....

14. He's not sure whether or not God exists.   ....

15. He claims that life is completely futile.   ....

16. She's a strong man-like woman.   ....

17. She has a sharp, bold tongue and temper.   ....

18. He has good taste in food.   ....

19. He's extremely handsome.   ....

20. He's coarse and uncouth.   ....

21. He's a beginner in his trade or profession.   ....

22. He is a student of words.   ....

23. He says he can see things that you can't.   ....

24. He's an authoritative judge and critic in some fine art.   ....

25. He collects stamps.   ....

ANSWERS: 1-atheist; 2-virtuoso; 3-numismatist; 4-esthete; 5-pedant; 6-judas; 7-coquette; 8-circe; 9-martinet; 10-egoist; 11-ascetic; 12-sycophant; 13-demagogue; 14-agnostic; 15-futilitarian; 16-amazon; 17-virago; 18-gourmet; 19-adonis; 20-vulgarian; 21-tyro; 22-philologist; 23-clairvoyant; 24-connoisseur; 25-philatelist

———

These are intensely human words about human characteristics, professions and avocations. They are warm to the fingertips, and for this reason, should be easy to learn.

WORDS FOR PHOBIAS AND MANIAS

We touched on a number of normal human characteristics in the last chapter. Now we turn to a few of the abnormalities of the human mind, to the words that particularize mental peculiarities, neuroses, phobias and mild or violent insanities.

I. Let us discuss five of the most common manias or mental diseases: kleptomania, pyromania, dipsomania, megalomania and monomania. You can perhaps get a more vivid view of the subject if you refresh your memory as to the approximate symptoms of those who are afflicted with these disorders.

1. The *pyromaniac* (pye-ro-may′-nee-ack) has a strange and morbid passion for fire. He will burn down a house with no slightest sense of malice, but merely because he is fascinated by the flames.

2. The *dipsomaniac* (dip-so-may′-nee-ack) has a compulsion to drink which he cannot control. His vice is more than a genial habit, of course. It is a psychological disease, and he must drink and get drunk whether he wants to or not.

3. The *megalomaniac* (meg-a-lo-may´-nee-ack) has a conviction that he is Napoleon or Caesar, or that he has enormous wealth. Or even that he is God. He is continually obsessed by delusions of grandeur.

4. The *monomaniac* (mon-o-may´-nee-ack) is unbalanced on just one subject, or a very limited range of subjects. On everything else except his own pet and particular delusion he may be completely sane.

5. The *kleptomaniac* (klep-toe-may´-nee-ack) has a compulsion to steal. The victim of this aberration may be wealthy and the object stolen may be worthless, and moreover this mentally unbalanced type of person never has any use for the stolen trinkets, nor any plans for their disposal. He just can't help taking them.

Please write in each one of the five blank spaces the type of mania that is described by each of the following sentences.

1. He can't take one drink and then stop.   ....

2. She is mentally deranged on one subject.   ....

3. She is apt to steal any little object that she sees.   ....

4. He imagines he is Hitler.   ....

5. It is dangerous to leave him alone with matches.   ....

ANSWERS: 1-dipsomaniac;   2-monomaniac;   3-kleptomaniac;
4-megalomaniac; 5-pyromaniac

II. What's your pet phobia? You haven't any? Don't be
too sure. How about your startled-turtle habit of duck-
ing under the bedclothes when the lightning crackles?
Or your shudders when a snake crosses your path? Or
possibly you edge away from the tops of tall buildings
because height makes you feel funny?

*If you are an average man you have, not one, but 2.21
phobias.*
If you are an average woman you have 3.55 phobias.

We will give you a list of the twelve most common ones.
We won't ask you to rehearse these words, or even to try
to remember them, as they will hardly ever be useful to
you, unless you should be a psychiatrist. But some of them
might be new to you, and it may interest you to see that
each one has a name.

Fear of thunder	ceraunophobia	(se-raw-no-foe′-bee-a)
Fear of lightning	astraphobia	(ass-tra-foe′-bee-a)
Fear of snakes	ophidiophobia	(o-fid-ee-o-foe′-bee-a)
Fear of darkness	nyctophobia	(nik-toe-foe′-bee-a)
Fear of heights	acrophobia	(ak-ro-foe′-bee-a)
Fear of fire	pyrophobia	(pye-ro-foe′-bee-a)
Fear of water	aquaphobia	(a-kwa-foe′-bee-a)
Fear of cats	ailurophobia	(ay-lyoo-ro-foe′-bee-a)
Fear of dogs	cynophobia	(sye-no-foe′-bee-a)
Fear of open spaces	agoraphobia	(ag-o-ra-foe′-bee-a)

| Fear of the number 13 | triskaideka-phobia | (triss-kye-dek-a-foe'-bee-a) |
| Fear of closed spaces | claustrophobia | (claw-stro-foe'-bee-a) |

Now forget them if you want to!

III. Here, however, are victims of four miscellaneous troubles that have to do with the mind and nerves:

The *hypochondriac* (hye-po-con'-dree-ack) is the person who is continually complaining about imaginary ills. A heart flutter means heart failure. A headache is a brain tumor. An upset stomach means gastric ulcers or cancer. The only real complaint is, of course, a morbid imagination. This trouble is called *hypochondria*.

The *amnesiac* (am-nee'-see-ack) suffers from loss of memory. This usually comes from a blow on the head, or some sudden shock. When this has happened the victim's mind becomes a complete blank as to his past. He can neither recall his family nor closest friends. In time, with modern treatment, there is usually a recovery. This disease is *amnesia*.

The *somnambulist* (som-nam'-byoo-list) walks in his sleep. He is troubled with *somnambulism*.

The *insomniac* (in-som'-nee-ack) is suffering from *insomnia*. That is, he is continually bothered with sleeplessness.

Which one of the above sufferers would be most likely to say the following?

1. "What a night. I didn't sleep a wink!" ....

2. "I walked around the room last night? Why I was fast asleep." ....

3. "Who am I? I've completely forgotten my name." ....

4. "I don't care what the doctor says. I know I've got heart trouble." ....

ANSWERS: 1-insomniac; 2-somnambulist; 3-amnesiac; 4-hypochondriac.

IV. The truly serious diseases of the mind take many forms. Here are four more victims. Of course, on many occasions throughout this book, we will inevitably be discussing many words you already know.

1. The *manic-depressive* (may-nik-de-press'-iv) has alternating moods of black depression and wild, uncontrollable exaltation or excitability. These changes are unpredictable and come without warning. Usually this type is not dangerous to others.

2. The *schizophrenic* (skiz-o-fren'-ik) is a split or divided personality. This is one of the commoner types of psychosis. The victim loses contact with his environment, lives in an unreal world of his own making, and often imagines he is someone else. *Schizophrenia* is largely a disease of youth.

3. The *melancholiac* (mel-an-co'-lee-ack), as the name implies, has fallen into a fixed condition of despondency. Unless *melancholia* is taken in hand and cured it is apt to lead to suicide.

4. The *paranoiac* (par-a-noy'-ack) has delusions of persecution. He imagines that people are trying to poison him, or that he is being pursued by enemies, and for this reason he is apt to be dangerous.

V. There are two mental idiosyncrasies that stand somewhat apart, as they rarely become calamities. They usually have their origins in childhood.

The possessor of the *Electra-complex* (ee-lek'-tra), always a girl, develops a vicious hostility towards her mother, with a corresponding and all-consuming love for her father.

The *Oedipus-complex* (ed'-i-pus) is the male version of this mental disorder. The victim is the familiar "mother's boy" who has been over-protected and over-babied, and so prevented from growing up emotionally. Here there is a strong hatred of the father. These two types rarely marry, or if they do they often have matrimonial troubles as the girl is always trying to find a husband who is the counterpart of her father, and the boy a wife who has all the virtues of his mother.

VI.

Disease	*Person*
1. kleptomania (klep-toe-may'-nee-a)	kleptomaniac

Disease	*Person*
2. pyromania (pye-ro-may´-nee-a)	pyromaniac
3. dipsomania (dip-so-may´-nee-a)	dipsomaniac
4. megalomania (meg-a-lo-may´-nee-a)	megalomaniac
5. monomania (mon-o-may´-nee-a)	monomaniac
6. hypochondria (hye-po-con´-dree-a)	hypochondriac
7. amnesia (am-nee´-see-a)	amnesiac
8. somnambulism (som-nam´-byoo-lizm)	somnambulist
9. insomnia (in-som´-nee-a)	insomniac
10. manic-depression (may-nik-de-presh´-un)	manic-depressive
11. schizophrenia (skiz-o-free´-nee-a)	schizophrene
12. Oedipus-complex (ed´-i-pus)	
13. Electra-complex (ee-lek´-tra)	
14. melancholia (mel-an-co´-lee-a)	melancholiac
15. paranoia (par-a-noy´-a)	paranoiac

VII. Can you fit the above words into their proper dictionary definitions?

    1. Mental derangement characterized by continued gloom and depression   ....

    2. Moods of violent excitement and mental depression   ....

    3. Loss or impairment of memory; morbid forgetfulness   ....

4. The act or state of walking and per-
   forming other actions during sleep   ....

5. An uncontrollable craving for alco-
   holic drink   ....

6. Morbid melancholy and anxiety
   about one's health   ....

7. Chronic mental unsoundness; de-
   mentia with delusions   ....

8. A complex involving an early and
   abnormal attachment of a girl for
   her father, with hostility towards
   her mother   ....

9. An insane or uncontrollable propen-
   sity to steal   ....

10. Insanity in which the subject thinks
    himself great or exalted   ....

11. Chronic inability to sleep   ....

12. Mental derangement confined to
    one idea   ....

13. An insane propensity to set fires   ....

14. A form of mental derangement
    characterized by a loss of touch with
    reality; a split personality   ....

15. The Electra-complex as applied to a
    boy's attachment to his mother   ....

16. Complete loss of memory and iden-
    tity   ....

17. A continual state of depression apt
    to lead to suicide   ....

ANSWERS: 1-melancholia; 2-manic-depression; 3-amnesia; 4-som-
nambulism; 5-dipsomania; 6-hypochondria; 7-para-
noia; 8-Electra-complex; 9-kleptomania; 10-mega-
lomania; 11-insomnia; 12-monomania; 13-pyromania;
14-schizophrenia; 15-Oedipus-complex; 16-amnesia;
17-melancholia

At some time in our book, particularly after such a
chapter as this, a few readers may think that we are advo-
cating the use of long and difficult words. But the words
we have given above happen to be the only ones that will
accurately describe the organic mental troubles and the
neurotic disorders that we have been discussing. There are
no substitutes.

But let this rule generally hold. Never, or at least almost
never, use a long word where a short one will do. Words,
as you well know, are to express your thoughts, not to
conceal them. The greatest poems and the greatest
speeches, whether it is Robert Burns' "My love is like a
red, red rose" or Patrick Henry's "Give me liberty or give
me death," all have the power and charm of simplicity.
Try to avoid the too frequent use of such Latin words as
juxtaposition, animadvert, salutation, recapitulate. They
tend to make your style heavy, dry, and pedantic. Short
Saxon words have force—*gift* instead of *donation; poor*
instead of *impecunious*. There is a simple beauty in *ship,
shop, walk, free, earth, mate, man, friend*. The Latin
words are important to know, but should be used with
discretion.

Simplicity and sincerity in everything, whether it be
manners or music or words, are always best.

WORDS ABOUT YOUR FEELINGS

During the last few chapters we have been dealing with all kinds of people—with their peculiarities, their mental quirks, their philosophies, their ideas. Now let us deal with ideas alone. Or shall we get more personal, and consider the terms that describe *your* thoughts, *your* feelings, *your* attitudes and emotions?

Consider these five words:

> nostalgia (noss-tal´-jee-a)
> satiated (say´-shee-ay-ted)
> benevolence (ben-ev´-o-lence)
> frustration (fruss-tray´-shun)
> lethargy (leth´-ar-jee)

Are any of these strange to you? Then here they are in sentences which should give a hint as to their meanings.

I. Study the following sentences carefully, especially noting the word in italics.

1. He was overcome with a wave of *nostalgia* whenever he thought of his boyhood years in Scotland.

2. The huge dinner left him *satiated*.

3. That morning he was at peace with the world; his attitude towards all mankind was one of *benevolence*.

4. All life, he claims, is *frustration*. The gods seem bent on mischievously thwarting his hopes and plans.

5. His illness left him in a state of *lethargy;* all ambition, interest, desire were gone.

II. Please take the italicized words in Section I and write them in their correct places in the spaces below so that each word will be opposite its proper definition.

1. .... Morbid stupor; state of apathy or indifference

2. .... Severe or morbid homesickness; a longing for past pleasant occurrences

3. .... Desire for well-being or comfort of others; charitableness

4. .... Filled beyond natural desire; glutted

5. .... Failure in attainment; defeat

ANSWERS: 1-lethargy; 2-nostalgia; 3-benevolence; 4-satiated; 5-frustration

———————

III. Consider the following group of words carefully and try to arrive at the meanings of those you don't already know.

enervated (en'-er-vay-ted)
weltschmerz (velt'-schmairts)

ennui (ahn'-wee)
compunction (com-punk'-shun)
antipathy (an-tip'-ath-ee)

1. His all-night vigil completely *enervated* him.

2. Adolescents are in general rather pessimistic about the future of humanity. This *weltschmerz* is a natural result of their changing minds and bodies.

3. Never had her life been so stagnant and empty. Never had she been so filled with *ennui*.

4. He had no *compunctions* about cheating his fellow man.

5. He had a violent *antipathy* to all political theories smacking, however faintly, of communism.

IV. Can you pair off each of the preceding words in italics with its correct definition below?

1. .... Literally, world pain; sadness from a gloomy view of world philosophy
2. .... An instinctive feeling of aversion or dislike
3. .... Self-reproach for wrong-doing; slight regret
4. .... Deprived of physical and nervous energy
5. .... A feeling of listless weariness resulting from satiety

ANSWERS: 1-weltschmerz; 2-antipathy; 3-compunction; 4-enervated; 5-ennui

V. Here is a new group for study in the same way.

> supercilious (syoo-per-sil'-ee-us)
> vindictive (vin-dik'-tiv)
> misogynist (miss-oj'-i-nist)
> misanthrope (miss'-an-thrope)
> vicariously (vye-cair'-ee-us-lee)

1. You are too *supercilious;* who do you think you are, anyway?

2. Be careful not to hurt her feelings, for she'll never forgive you. You know how *vindictive* some women are.

3. Queer chap—I think he's a *misogynist*. That's probably why he never married.

4. At heart he's a *misanthrope*. No wonder he has no friends.

5. Since his accident he has been unable to take part in the sports that he used to love. Now he reads the sports page and enjoys tennis, golf, and baseball *vicariously*.

VI. Write each of the words in italics in Section V into the spaces allowed in Section VI. Match the word to the definition ahead of it if you can.

1. Manner of experiencing something indirectly instead of directly   ....

2. A hater of mankind   ....

3. A hater of women ....

4. Disposed to revenge; retaliatory ....

5. Lofty with pride; haughtily contemptuous ....

ANSWERS: 1-vicariously; 2-misanthrope; 3-misogynist; 4-vindictive; 5-supercilious

---

VII. The pronunciations of the foregoing words are not always easy to remember. Pronounce them over again out loud.

1. lethargy	6. weltschmerz	11. vicariously
2. nostalgia	7. antipathy	12. misanthrope
3. benevolence	8. compunction	13. misogynist
4. satiated	9. enervated	14. vindictive
5. frustration	10. ennui	15. supercilious

VIII. Does each pair of the following words have the same meaning, or are they opposed in meaning? Write *s* or *o*, according to your idea.

1. lethargy	....	energy
2. nostalgia	....	home-sickness
3. benevolence	....	malevolence
4. satiated	....	full
5. frustration	....	satisfaction

6. weltschmerz	....	happiness
7. antipathy	....	sympathy
8. compunctions	....	scruples
9. enervated	....	tired
10. ennui	....	boredom
11. vicariously	....	actually
12. misanthrope	....	philanthropist
13. misogynist	....	Lothario
14. vindictive	....	forgiving
15. supercilious	....	diffident

ANSWERS: 1-0; 2-s; 3-0; 4-s; 5-0; 6-0; 7-0; 8-s; 9-s;
10-s; 11-0; 12-0; 13-0; 14-0; 15-0

IX. Give a different part of speech, as required.

1. Change *lethargy* to an adjective to fit into the following phrase: A .... attitude.

2. *Nostalgia* to an adjective: A .... feeling.

3. *Benevolence* to an adverb: He beamed ....

4. *Satiated* to a negative adjective: He is an .... reader.

5. *Satiated* to a noun (not ending in *ation*): I've had a .... of motion pictures.

6. *Frustration* to a verb: Why do you try to .... me?

7. *Antipathy* to an adjective: I am .... to such ideas.

8. *Enervated* to a noun: The cause of his ....

9. *Vicariously* to an adjective: A .... thrill.

10. *Misanthrope* to another noun denoting the person: He is a ....

11. *Misanthrope* to a noun denoting the philosophy: What is the cause of his ....?

12. *Misogynist* to a noun denoting the philosophy: What is the cause of his ....?

13. *Vindictive* to a noun: I dislike him mainly for his ....

14. *Supercilious* to a noun: Your .... will make you lose many friends.

ANSWERS: 1-lethargic (leth-ar'-jik); 2-nostalgic (noss-tal'-jik); 3-benevolently (ben-ev'-o-lent-lee); 4-insatiable (in-say'-shee-a-bul); 5-satiety (sa-tye'-e-tee); 6-frustrate (fruss'-trate); 7-antipathetic (an-ti-pa-thet'-ik); 8-enervation (en-er-vay'-shun); 9-vicarious (vye-cair'-ee-us); 10-misanthropist (miss-an'-thro-pist); 11-misanthropy (miss-an'-thro-pee); 12-misogyny (miss-oj'-i-nee) 13-vindictiveness (vin-dik'-tiv-ness); 14-superciliousness (syoo-per-sil'-ee-us-ness)

These words may not have been unknown to you. But you can see that if they should be completely foreign to a person, he would have to fumble with any ideas related to these subjects, for these words express certain specific ideas, compactly, richly, effectively, and as no other words could.

Once a person knows the proper words, the ideas connected with them become simple and understandable. With a well-stocked arsenal of words to do your command you can become a more powerful and influential thinker, writer, and speaker.

WORDS THAT END IN "OLOGY"

Traveling at the rate of 186,000 miles a second a ray of light started towards the earth with the message that a star had exploded somewhere in space. Thirteen centuries passed by before it arrived. Goethe, Shakespeare, Galileo and King Arthur's Court all came and went. Napoleon strode over Europe like a colossus, lost his kingdom and died. America was discovered. Great wars began and ceased and then began again, while this glimmer of light was racing on its way to tell our astronomers of a world-shaking catastrophe that had happened in the constellation of Hercules.

This message was read and understood. And that is the triumph of the mind of man.

His intellect can weigh the sun and measure the heat from the farthest star. His eyes can see a billion miles into space and they can also explore the infinitesimal world of electrons. Man has struggled for his knowledge of medicine and archaeology and geology and the multitude of sciences and we, by the miracle of words, can open some of these doors, and if they are so much as opened we may be tempted to go farther.

I. The Field of Human Knowledge.

1. *Anthropology* (an-thro-pol'-o-jee): This word we
   have had before and you will recognize it as "the
   science of mankind" in general, his habits, history,
   distribution, culture. The masters of this field
   would be *anthropologists* (an-thro-pol'-o-jists).

2. *Geology* (jee-ol'-o-jee): The meaning of this word
   is made crystal clear when we know that the "geo"
   comes from the Greek word *ge* which stands for
   "earth," and that this stem plus the combining
   form "logy" gives us "the science or knowledge of
   the earth." There are a whole host of "geologies,"
   but the common meaning refers to the science that
   deals with the structure of our earth, the operation
   of its forces and the history of all these. The secrets
   of the earth are ferreted out by *geologists* (jee-ol'-o-
   jists).

3. *Archaeology* (ar-kee-ol'-o-jee): This can almost be
   called the science of antiquities. It deals with the
   old records that men leave in such forms as buildings and pottery and in the physical remains of
   their industries. The key to the language of the
   Aztecs of ancient Mexico, for example, has not been
   fully discovered but *archaeologists* (ar-kee-ol'-o-
   jists) can learn much of the story of this race from
   the ruins they left. (Greek: *arche,* "beginning," and
   therefore "the study of beginnings.")

4. *Embryology* (em-bree-ol'-o-jee): As we know, in
   the early stages of pre-natal development, the
   unborn child is called an *embryo*. Once more the

Greeks can help us, for *en* in that language means "in" and *bryo* "swell," or, literally, to swell inside, which is just what happens in pregnancy. An *embryologist* (em-bree-ol'-o-jist) is a scientist who deals with the beginnings of life.

5. *Entomology* (en-toe-mol'-o-jee): When you know that *entomon* in Greek means "insect" the rest is easy to guess. The *entomologists* (en-toe-mol'-o-jists) have given to our world a wealth of knowledge about the home life, sex habits and political and social customs of bees, ants, butterflies and other members of the tiny race.

6. *Ethnology* (eth-nol'-o-jee): White men, brown men, black men, yellow men. What is their history? Where did they come from? Where do they live? How do they differ in mind, culture, characteristics? These are problems for the *ethnologist* (eth-nol'-o-jist) to solve. These words are from the Greek *ethnos* meaning "race."

7. *Etymology* (et-i-mol'-o-jee): You will recall that this is the study of the history and origin of words.

8. *Ornithology* (or-ni-thol'-o-jee): If you are told that *ornis* is the Greek term for "bird" you can find your own meaning. The lives and habits of eagles and whippoorwills, tanagers and sparrows, hawks and sea gulls—the study of this is in the hands of the *ornithologists* (or-ni-thol'-o-jists).

9. *Philology* (fil-ol'-o-jee): This word we are already familiar with. The *philologist* (fil-ol'-o-jist) is the all-embracing scientist who covers the entire field of words and language.

10. *Psychology* (sye-kol'-o-jee): Once more let's leaf over the pages of our Greek lexicon, and we find *psyche* "soul," "mind." So the *psychologist* (sye-kol'-o-jist) is an authority on the human mind and on human behavior in all of its aspects.

II.   *The Field*   *The Student*

1. anthropology   anthropologist
2. geology   geologist
3. archaeology   archaeologist
4. embryology   embryologist
5. entomology   entomologist
6. ethnology   ethnologist
7. etymology   etymologist
8. ornithology   ornithologist
9. philology   philologist
10. psychology   psychologist

III. If you wished the answer to each of the following questions, to which of the scholars and specialists in Section II would you turn for your information?

1. What does the unborn baby look like during the third week of its development?   ....

2. How many Mayan ruins are there in Central America?   ....

3. What makes human beings behave the way they do?   ....

4. What kind of rock is found in Tennessee? ....

5. Is it true that the owl is wiser than other birds? ....

6. What did the men of the Stone Age look like? ....

7. What is the life span of an ant? ....

8. What is the derivation or origin of the word *boycott?* ....

9. How many different languages are spoken in Europe? ....

10. Where are the yellow races found in greatest abundance? ....

ANSWERS: 1-embryologist; 2-archaeologist; 3-psychologist; 4-geologist; 5-ornithologist; 6-anthropologist; 7-entomologist; 8-etymologist; 9-philologist; 10-ethnologist

There are so many things you can do with these words. Say them aloud. That is the first step towards making them your own. If you aren't absolutely sure of how to pronounce them you won't dare to use them.

Try spelling them. Get a friend or a member of your family to help you if you like. Each such step is a clincher that helps hold the word more firmly in your mind.

Experiment with the etymologies that have been recorded here. The Greek stem *ge* means earth. How easy it is then to read the meaning of *ge*ography, *ge*opolitics.

Arche, we have found, means "beginning." Then we can realize what an "archetype" would be.

Psyche, the dictionaries tell us, means "soul" or "mind." Then compare "psychic," "psychiatry," "psychoanalysis."

Once a person learns that words have cousins and uncles and aunts without number—that there is a kinship between them all—then his vocabulary will grow apace.

WORDS FOR HUMAN TRAITS

Men and women have so many forms of conduct, and such a multitude of varied characteristics and points of view that they have inspired a host of descriptive adjectives. We will introduce the new words first in a series of simple sentences where the context will give at least a hint as to the meanings of those terms that are not already familiar to the reader.

I. 1. The *loquacious* (lo-kway'-shus) girl talks incessantly.

2. The *gullible* (gull'-i-bul) housewife believes everything a canvasser tells her.

3. The *suave* (swahv) talker can persuade you that black is white.

4. The *pompous* (pom'-pus) person seems overwhelmed with a sense of his own importance.

5. The *esthetic* (ess-thet'-ik) artist has dedicated his life to beauty.

6. The *taciturn* (tass'-i-turn) husband answers his wife in grunts and monosyllables.

7. The *opinionated* (o-pin'-yun-ay-ted) fool has a mind

so finally made up that neither hell nor high water can make him change it.

8. The *phlegmatic* (fleg-mat'-ik) person can't get excited over anything.

9. The *erudite* (air'-oo-dite) man has learned views.

10. The *complacent* (com-play'-sent) fellow is sure that everything is going to come out all right.

11. The *punctilious* (punk-til'-ee-us) hostess worries if so much as one fork is out of place on her perfectly set table.

12. The *indefatigable* (in-de-fat'-i-ga-bul) worker seems capable of getting along on four hours' sleep a day.

13. The *vapid* (vap'-id) talker's conversation is completely meaningless.

14. The *iconoclastic* (eye-con-o-class'-tik) critic carps at such institutions as government, marriage, and religion.

15. The *misanthropic* (miss-an-throp'-ik) cynic hates the world and everybody in it.

16. The *puerile* (pyoo'-er-ill) practical joker may have grown up physically but is still a child emotionally.

17. The *ascetic* (a-set'-ik) person lives in a hut and likes it.

II. The brief description of the people in Part I may not be enough to give you a clue to the meanings of such words as may be new to you. But try, anyway, to match the words in italics above with the definitions that follow.

1. Completely self-satisfied and contented ....
2. Smooth and pleasant in manner; bland; gracious

   ....

3. Not easily perturbed; calm; indifferent ....
4. One who assails traditional beliefs ....
5. Simple; credulous; easily deceived ....
6. Marked by assumed importance; pretentiousness

   ....

7. Appreciating or loving the beautiful; artistic

   ....

8. Characteristic of childhood; juvenile; immature

   ....

9. Very learned; scholarly ....
10. Practicing extreme abstinence and devotion; self-denying

    ....

11. Terribly talkative; garrulous ....
12. Habitually silent or reserved ....
13. Unduly attached to one's own opinions; obstinate

    ....

14. Not exhausted by labor or exercise; unflagging

    ....

15. One who hates mankind ....
16. Very exact in the observance of forms of etiquette or ceremony

    ....

17. Having lost sparkling quality and flavor; flat; dull; insipid

    ....

ANSWERS: 1-complacent; 2-suave; 3-phlegmatic; 4-iconoclastic; 5-gullible; 6-pompous; 7-esthetic; 8-puerile; 9-erudite; 10-ascetic; 11-loquacious; 12-taciturn; 13-opinionated; 14-indefatigable; 15-misanthrope; 16-punctilious; 17-vapid

---

III. Each phrase below describes an adjective you have just had. Fill in every blank space with the adjective that fits the descriptive phrase. Just to make it a little harder for you, several adjectives will be called for more than once.

1. Emotionally sluggish
   ....

2. Practicing self-denial
   ....

3. Disinclined to conversation
   ....

4. Having an antipathy for mankind ....

5. Easily duped ....

6. Insipid ....

7. Scholarly ....

8. Talkative ....

9. Precise in the observance of forms or ceremonies
   ....

10. Ostentatious and self-important ....

11. Inane ....

12. Responsive to beauty
    ....

13. The attitude of one who attacks cherished beliefs as shams ....

14. Childish ....

15. Polished in manner
    ....

16. Stubbornly set in opinions ....

17. Self-satisfied ....

18. The attitude of a person who attacks established traditions ....

19. Having an aversion for the human race ....

20. Tireless ....

21. Urbanely persuasive ....

22. Contented with things as they are ....

ANSWERS: 1-phlegmatic; 2-ascetic; 3-taciturn; 4-misanthropic; 5-gullible; 6-vapid; 7-erudite; 8-loquacious; 9-punctilious; 10-pompous; 11-vapid; 12-esthetic; 13-iconoclastic; 14-puerile; 15-suave; 16-opinionated; 17-complacent; 18-iconoclasm; 19-misanthropic; 20-indefatigable; 21-suave; 22-complacent

---

IV. Now test your understanding of these 17 words once more by marking each of the following statements "true" or "false."

1. Talkative women are called *loquacious*.

2. Country yokels are as a rule *suave*.

3. Truck drivers are usually *esthetic*.

4. Enthusiastic people are usually *taciturn*.

5. The more just a man is the more *opinionated* he becomes.

6. *Phlegmatic* people usually lose their heads in an emergency.

7. *Pomposity* is usually amusing.

8. College professors are often *erudite*.

9. Smug people are never *complacent*.

10. *Punctilious* people are sticklers for form.

11. The beaver is an *indefatigable* worker.

12. The conversation of a conceited bore is usually *vapid*.

13. The attitude of a Communist towards American institutions is *iconoclastic*.

14. A *misanthrope* loves his fellow men.

15. *Puerility* in a man is a characteristic of maturity.

16. The *ascetic* is given to sensuality.

17. A young child is apt to be *gullible*.

ANSWERS: 1-true; 2-false; 3-false; 4-false; 5-false; 6-false; 7-true; 8-true; 9-false; 10-true; 11-true; 12-true; 13-true; 14-false; 15-false; 16-false; 17-true

———

V. The 17 adjectives that we have been considering are directly opposite in meaning to the 17 words or phrases in this section. "Loquacious" for instance is opposite in meaning to, or the "antonym" of, "taciturn." Can you write the other antonyms in their correct places?

1. taciturn .... 6. lazy ....

2. easily swayed .... 7. dissatisfied ....

3. ignorant .... 8. conservative ....

4. philanthropic .... 9. mature ....

5. blind to beauty .... 10. careless of etiquette ....

11. voluptuous   ....   15. high-strung   ....

12. uncivil, churlish ....   16. hard to cheat   ....

13. modest   ....   17. clever and interesting

14. loquacious   ....

ANSWERS: 1-loquacious; 2-opinionated; 3-erudite; 4-misanthrop-
ic; 5-esthetic; 6-indefatigable; 7-complacent; 8-icono-
clastic; 9-puerile; 10-punctilious; 11-ascetic; 12-suave;
13-pompous; 14-taciturn; 15-phlegmatic; 16-gullible;
17-vapid

VI. Let's test your wits again. The game should be getting easier. Check the one correct answer out of three
in each division.

1. Loquacity is an inordinate amount of
   a. singing
   b. attention to details
   c. talking
2. Gullible people fall easy prey to
   a. chauvinists
   b. salesmen
   c. teachers
3. Suave people are experts at
   a. trickery
   b. love
   c. persuasiveness
4. Pomposity probably comes from
   a. fear
   b. obesity
   c. vanity

5. Most likely to be esthetic is an
    a. electrician
    b. aviator
    c. artist

6. Taciturnity would likely be found in people who are
    a. excitable
    b. public speakers
    c. hermits

7. Opinionated assertions may likely lead to
    a. marriage
    b. arguments
    c. truth

8. A phlegmatic person
    a. sheds tears at an emotional play
    b. goes to pieces in a crisis
    c. does not become enthusiastic over things

9. Erudite men are most interested in
    a. scholarly books
    b. light fiction
    c. comic strips

10. People who are complacent about their jobs will
    a. take it easy
    b. worry about their future
    c. keep an eye on the help wanted ads

11. A punctilious person is a stickler for
    a. originality
    b. courage
    c. good manners

12. To be indefatigable, one usually needs a great amount of
    a. money
    b. energy
    c. education

13. Vapid people are
    a. bores
    b. successful
    c. quarrelsome

14. Iconoclasts are opposed to
    a. change
    b. tradition
    c. reform

15. A misanthrope dislikes
    a. people
    b. good food
    c. literature

16. Men are most likely to be puerile when
    a. they don't get their own way
    b. they are reading
    c. they are eating

17. Most ascetics would prefer to be
    a. roustabouts
    b. hermits
    c. great lovers

ANSWERS: 1-c; 2-b; 3-c; 4-c; 5-c; 6-c; 7-b; 8-c; 9-a; 10-a; 11-c; 12-b; 13-a; 14-b; 15-a; 16-a; 17-b

VII. The stories behind the words in this chapter. If several word histories are omitted from the list it is because they are uninteresting and have little bearing on the meanings of the English derivatives:

Suave: The Latin word *suavis* is identical with ours, meaning sweet, gracious, pleasant.

Iconoclastic: Greek *eikon*—"idol"; *klao*—"break." An "iconoclast," then, is a breaker of idols, or, in the modern sense, a breaker of traditions.

Pompous: Latin *pomposus*—"stately."

Esthetic: The Greek word *aisthetikos* "perceptive" becomes refined in our language until it refers to the finer feelings and finer perceptions in the field of art and culture.

Puerile: Of course is from the Latin, *puer* "boy." When a man is "puerile" he is acting like a child.

Ascetic: Greek *asketikos,* which has to do with exercise. Possibly through the discipline required in exercise it came to mean moral discipline.

Loquacious: Is a simple word to trace from the Latin, *loquor,* meaning "speak."

Taciturn: Latin *tacere*—"to be silent."

Opinionated: From Latin *opinio*—"thought" or "opinion." "Opinionated" means too well provided with opinions or stubborn in ideas.

Indefatigable: Latin, *in*—"not" and *defatigare*—"to tire out."

Punctilious: From the Latin *punctum,* or "point." "Punctilious" is used, in our language, to refer to someone who is very attentive to fine points. "Punctual" derives from the same Latin word.

Vapid: This and the Latin word *vapidus* both mean "insipid."

We have tried purposely in this book to save the reader the trouble of going to the dictionary. But it is hardly necessary for us to remind the student of words that he will find the dictionary habit an invaluable one to form. It is only in this way that one can get a real feeling for words and learn to know the fine distinctions between meanings.

How about looking up the three useful but tricky words, *punctilious, meticulous* and *scrupulous?* Can you distinguish between them? There are interesting word histories behind them and it will be good practice to look them up in your dictionary.

WORDS FOR HUMAN FAULTS

Have you ever met the gay young bachelor type whose life seems to be one *peccadillo* after another? Does such a one have to be a man of some wealth, or can he follow his manner of life in the midst of *penury*? Do his successes with the opposite sex tend to give him a touch of *megalomania*? His life is certainly an interesting one: that is, if you consider that one *imbroglio* after another makes for interest. Just listen to him talk. His *braggadocio* may entertain his younger acquaintances, but it certainly becomes tiresome to his older friends!

I. Pronounce each word carefully:

1. peccadillo (pek-a-dill'-o)
2. penury (pen'-you-ree)
3. megalomania (meg-a-lo-may'-nee-a)
4. imbroglio (im-bro'-lyo)
5. braggadocio (brag-a-doe'-shee-o)

From an analysis of the preceding paragraph can you fit the five words into the following definitions?

1. A complicated and embarrassing situation   ....

2. A slight sin   ....

3. Empty boasting   ....

4. Abject poverty   ....

5. Grandiose delusions of one's own importance   ....

ANSWERS: 1-imbroglio; 2-peccadillo; 3-braggadocio; 4-penury; 5-megalomania

---

II. Now for another group. What kind of person are you? Do you think money is a *panacea?* Do you feel your life has been a *fiasco?* What are some of your *idiosyncrasies?* Do you tend to *rationalize* rather than face the truth? Are there *anomalies* in your life that you would like to see removed? The answers to these questions can often reveal a number of interesting things about a person's character.

1. panacea (pan-a-see'-a)

2. fiasco (fee-ass'-co)

3. idiosyncrasy (id-ee-o-sin'-kra-see)

4. rationalize (rash'-un-al-ize)

5. anomaly (a-nom'-a-lee)

1. Something that is irregular or incon-
   sistent.   ....

2. A cure for all evils.   ....

3. A miserable and ridiculous failure.   ....

4. To reason out and invent a worthy
   motive for a discreditable act.   ....

5. A characteristic peculiarity.   ....

ANSWERS: 1-anomaly; 2-panacea; 3-fiasco; 4-rationalize; 5-idio-
         syncrasy

III. Do you by chance have a neurotic friend who is so
lazy that he tends to *malinger*? Or one who belongs
to the *elite* and looks down a social nose at the *par-
venus*? The conversation of such a person is apt to be
banal, certainly not as interesting as that of the *intelligentsia*. Or have you ever been up against a politician
who resorts to *jingoism* and *chicanery* because he cannot gain his end by honest means?

Read the following seven words out loud:

1. malinger (ma-ling´-ger)

2. elite (ay-leet´)

3. parvenu (par´-ve-nyoo)

4. jingoism (jing´-go-izm)

5. intelligentsia (in-tell-i-jent´-see-a)

6. chicanery (shi-kay´-ner-ee)

7. banal (bay´-nal)

Can you pair off the preceding words with the definitions that follow?

1. The choicest part of society, or flower of an army ....

2. One who has suddenly attained wealth beyond his birth or worth. Usually used derogatively ....

3. To feign sickness to shirk work or duty ....

4. Favoring a demonstrative foreign policy ....

5. The intelligent and educated classes ....

6. Mean, petty trickery ....

7. Commonplace; trivial ....

ANSWERS: 1-elite; 2-parvenu; 3-malinger; 4-jingoism; 5-intelligentsia; 6-chicanery; 7-banal

---

IV. Now is a good time to read these words aloud, and so make sure that you can pronounce them. Otherwise you will never use them in conversation.

1. peccadillo
2. penury
3. megalomania
4. imbroglio
5. braggadocio
6. panacea
7. fiasco
8. idiosyncrasy
9. rationalize
10. anomaly
11. elite
12. jingoism
13. intelligentsia
14. malinger
15. chicanery
16. banal
17. parvenu

Do you remember what these words mean? Try to fill in the proper word after each of the following synonymous phrases.

1. Extreme poverty or want ....

2. The best socially or intellectually ....

3. A complete or humiliating failure ....

4. Trickery ....

5. To feign illness in order to escape work ....

6. To interpret in reasonable manner ....

7. A deviation from type; an irregularity ....

8. A pretended remedy for all diseases ....

9. Favoring a demonstrative foreign policy ....

10. Educated and intellectual people ....

11. Ordinary; dull ....

12. Delusions of grandeur ....

13. Pretentious boasting ....

14. A slight or trifling sin ....

15. A troublesome complication of affairs ....

16. A characteristic peculiarity ....

17. A mushroom aristocrat ....

ANSWERS: 1-penury; 2-elite; 3-fiasco; 4-chicanery; 5-malinger; 6-rationalize; 7-anomaly; 8-panacea; 9-jingoistic; 10-intelligentsia; 11-banal; 12-megalomania; 13-braggadocio; 14-peccadillo; 15-imbroglio; 16-idiosyncrasy; 17-parvenu

V. Which word does each of the following phrases bring to mind?

1. Down with the foreigners! ....

2. It was all right to steal because my family were starving. ....

3. The great South Sea Bubble. ....

4. We all want peace and get war. ....

5. The people in *Who's Who*. ....

6. A boy pretends he's sick to get out of school. ....

7. The economic condition of the population of the slums. ....

8. I call what he did only a mild indiscretion. ....

9. Misleading advertising. ....

10. Europe has been in one for years. ....

11. Hitler. ....

12. He has a slight hesitation in his speech. ....

13. He is dull and uninteresting in his conversation. ....

ANSWERS: 1-jingoism; 2-rationalization; 3-fiasco; 4-anomaly; 5-elite; 6-malinger; 7-penury; 8-peccadillo; 9-chicanery; 10-imbroglio; 11-megalomaniac; 12-idiosyncrasy; 13-banal

VI. How other people have used some of these words:

1. As Professor Owen has remarked, there is no greater *anomaly* in nature than a bird that cannot fly.

    (DARWIN)

2. Owing to the disunion of the Fenians themselves, the rigor of the administration, and the treachery of informers, the (Irish) rebellion was a *fiasco*.

    (*The Encyclopaedia Britannica*)

3. *Idiosyncrasies* are, however, frequent; thus we find that one person has an exceptional memory for sounds, another for colors, another for forms.

    (*The Encyclopaedia Britannica*)

4. The chemists pretended it was the philosopher's stone, the physicians that it was an infallible *panacea*.

    (T. WHARTON)

5. The Koran attaches much importance to prayer—a fact which is somewhat *anomalous* in a system of religion so essentially fatalistic. (SPENCER)

6. Men who by legal *chicanery* cheat others out of their property. (HERBERT SPENCER)

7. Who doesn't forgive? The virtuous Mrs. Grundy. She remembers her neighbors' *peccadilloes* to the third and fourth generations. (THACKERAY)

8. I have always observed through life that your *parvenu* it is who stickles for what he calls the genteel, and has the most squeamish abhorrence for what is frank and natural. (THACKERAY)

9. 'Tis low ebb with his accusers when such *peccadilloes*
as these are put in to swell the charge.

(BISHOP OF ATTERBURY)

You will find it good practice if you will start looking
for these words in your daily reading. You may be surprised how often they will occur, not because they are so
popular, but principally for the reason that your mind
is now set to recognize them.

You are now halfway through this book.

How is your work going? Do you feel you are making
progress? Here are a few suggestions that may increase
your speed.

Try laying out a simple, definite but not over-ambitious
plan for your daily study, if you haven't already done so.
Fix a date when you think you can reasonably finish the
volume, and be sure to schedule a daily delivery of achieve-
ment. It will be wise not to make your plan overhard, as
you may then fall behind and that is always discouraging.
If you can choose a fixed time each day for this study, that
will be helpful. But if that should be impractical, then
learn the fine art of using your spare moments. John
Erskine, the famous author, trained himself to use all
those minutes of the day that other people waste, and during these periods of salvaged time he wrote most of his
novels.

Above all, make this present study a habit, like getting
dressed or undressed, combing your hair or brushing your
teeth, and it will soon become so much a part of your life
that you will feel guilty if you skip a single time.

And here is a rule that busy men have found invaluable. Always plan your next day's work the night before.

16. Sixteenth Day

YOU HELP TO CREATE THE AMERICAN LANGUAGE

We have now come to an interval, a halfway mark, in our consideration of words.

We can take a little time out to discuss the matter of who owns this language that we have been studying.

Well, you own it. And you. And you. The English language belongs to you. You made it. You are making it every day. You have invented upwards of 600,000 usable English words, minus those that have been taken over from other languages. But even these were adopted by you. You have devised the queer spellings of English words. You have determined their pronunciations.

In English we are dealing with an inexact art. Not an exact science. Even the mistakes of English are human. Some of our fantastic spellings in this book that you hold in your hand are due merely to the errors of ignorant typesetters who lived centuries ago. We have merely preserved and honored their misspellings. Pronunciations and meanings are frequently modified with just as little reason.

How then, specifically, do you control the language? In this way.

During this present year about five thousand new words will come into our language.

Intense and dramatic times such as these are always prolific in breeding new words.

The scholars won't mint or invent these new words. They will just pop up. The scholars will have nothing whatsoever to say about how they shall be pronounced or spelled, or as to what they mean. They will be pronounced and spelled and defined pretty much as the public pleases. If you were to ask the editor of the Funk & Wagnall's New Standard Dictionary or of Webster's or the Oxford or of any other, "Who decides about these new words?" this editor would answer, "You do," meaning, of course, the many millions of "you" who use our language.

Let's take a case in point. The new invention *television* came in and some one of you thought up the word *telecast* as a parallel term to *broadcast*. The experts of the broadcasting chains are bitterly opposed to the term. Scholars call it a bastard type of word, half from the Greek, *tele,* meaning, as you know, "far away," and half from the English word *cast,* but *telecast* it's going to be, just the same, like it or not, thanks to the common people who have already included it in the current coin of their conversation.

In similar fashion—that is, by usage—old words completely change their meanings, nice words become coarse, and coarse become respectable.

Slang, for instance, is a good example of the latter move on the part of words.

A great mass of our language was once the slang of the various Gas House Districts of the world. A large part of it came from over the railroad tracks. Purists and high-brows protested and fulminated against it, but little by little common usage made many of these words so respectable that the scholars were willing to use them and were forced to include them in the dictionaries.

Around 250 years ago, for example, Dean Swift was kicking (slang) at the then current use of such slang words as *bubble, sham, bully, hips,* as "a disgrace to our language." Now you and I use them very happily. Let us recite a few more that were once slang: *gin, boycott, cab, greenhorn, hoax, jingoist.*

You see the masses kept on using these words until they *had* to be included in our lexicons. And conversely, when these or any other words such as those that are included in this volume stop being commonly used, they will die and drop out of our dictionary. *You* will determine this, and our lexicographers will have nothing to do about it.

Now by just what methods did such words, for instance, as you have been working with in this book, ever get into the dictionary?

This is the way. The technique may be interesting to you.

Somebody writes in and asks the dictionary publisher about an apparently new word, or a staff reader discovers it among the Niagara of words pouring out from the presses of the world. So they first check it to find if it really *is* new. They look for it in all the standard English reference works that have come out during the last two centuries. If they don't find it there, and since it might be foreign, they leaf through glossaries of Sanskrit, Maori,

Hansa, Urdu, Hebrew, Afrikander and all the languages, ancient and modern, that were spawned by the Tower of Babel. If it still evades them they take a look at the trade and professional dictionaries, say those of lace-making, politics, petroleum, draperies, botany and others too many to count.

By this time it's a foxy word that's going to fool them!

If the term proves itself as new they put it on file for about five years.

Now how does it get in?

They watch its *use* by the people during the probationary period. Authors may take it up. Inquiries may come to the office about its meaning. At the end of the interval the record of the neophyte is added up and *if its score shows a sufficient popular demand,* the word goes into the dictionary. Thus and no otherwise.

Now, how is it *defined?* To be concrete, how were the definitions of the words in the last chapter originally determined upon?

As the researchers watch a new word in use they copy the actual sentences in which the word appears. When a given dictionary editor finally sits down to make up his definition he will have in front of him a stack of cards containing sentences that give the word and the context. The meaning, or the meanings, that he gives the word will be based, *not in any way on his own opinion,* but upon the sheaf of popular quotations he finds in front of him. His authority, and the authority of the dictionary, then, lie, not in this editor's particular scholarship, but in *your* whim and in the whim of the other millions who have invented, pronounced, spelled and defined the word for him.

And so when we study the English language we are studying our own handiwork. It is as democratic as our national institutions and the so-called "common people" are its inexhaustible source. The final authority for English rests, not with some dictionary House of Lords, but with the House of Commons, and this is what gives our language its vitality, force and rich humanity, and is what helps to make it such a thrilling study.

17. Seventeenth Day

TEST YOUR PROGRESS

At this point you are going to get a sudden surprise test that will give you a yardstick by which you can measure, in some fashion, the success you are having in keeping new words in your mind.

We are going to take a single chapter out of the past and try to see how good your memory is.

I. Here are the fifteen words you had in Chapter 12:

lethargy	enervated
nostalgia	ennui
benevolence	vicariously
satiated	misanthrope
frustration	misogynist
weltschmerz	vindictive
antipathy	supercilious
compunction	

II. Write the proper words, as best you can, next to each of the following synonyms or synonymous phrases. Just to make it a little harder, some of the words will be repeated.

1. Aversion ....

2. Exhausted ....

3. Indirect or second-hand ....

4. Sluggishness ....

5. Tedium ....

6. Weariness of life; sentimental
   pessimism ....

7. Remorseful feeling ....

8. Revengeful ....

9. Aversion; dislike ....

10. Deprived of vitality ....

11. Longing for the past ....

12. Woman-hater ....

13. Unpleasantly superior ....

14. Futility, obstruction ....

15. Philosophical and emotional world-
    sorrow ....

16. Magnanimity ....

17. Regret for wrong-doing ....

18. Filled full ....

ANSWERS: 1-antipathy; 2-enervated; 3-vicarious; 4-lethargy; 5-en-
nui; 6-weltschmerz; 7-compunction; 8-vindictive; 9-
antipathy; 10-enervated; 11-nostalgia; 12-misogynist;
13-supercilious; 14-frustration; 15-weltschmerz; 16-
benevolence; 17-compunction; 18-satiated

III. In the next exercise we will make certain statements, each of which will include one of the fifteen review words. In some cases the statements will be correct, in others incorrect. Record your opinion by writing "true" or "false" in the space at the end of each sentence.

1. *Misanthropes* have an *antipathy* toward their fellow men. ....

2. Staying up all night is very *enervating*. ....

3. One can get a *vicarious* thrill from the movies. ....

4. People on the qui vive are usually *lethargic*. ....

5. Young girls are filled with *ennui* at their first party. ....

6. Optimistic people are weighed down with *weltschmerz*. ....

7. A military conqueror has strong *compunctions* about taking other people's land. ....

8. *Vindictiveness* is an exceedingly attractive trait. ....

9. *Nostalgia* is a prevalent ill among young people who are away from home for the first time. ....

10. Haters of women are called *misogynists*. ....

11. The intelligent members of motion-picture audiences have had a *satiety* of the double feature. ....

12. The depression generation experienced poignant *frustration*. ....

13. Ivan the Terrible, Emperor of Russia,
    was famous for his great *benevolence*.   ....

14. Shy girls are *supercilious*.   ....

ANSWERS: 1-true; 2-true; 3-true; 4-false; 5-false; 6-false; 7-false;
8-false; 9-true; 10-true; 11-true; 12-true; 13-false; 14-false

---

IV. In this section, twelve words or phrases are given.
Each one is opposite in meaning to one of the words that
are the subject of this chapter. Try to fill in each blank
space with one of the words you have just been studying
that will be opposite in meaning to the printed word or
phrase. We are purposely omitting three of the fifteen
words to eliminate the possibility of guess-work. Occasionally a different part of speech will be required. That is, you
may have to change *antipathy*, let's say, from a noun to an
adjective. Remember, all the words you write in must be
antonyms, or opposites in meaning.

1. Joy in living   ....

2. Exhilaration   ....

3. Chivalry   ....

4. Forgivingness   ....

5. Sympathy   ....

6. First-hand experience   ....

7. Keen interest   ....

8. Heartlessness   ....

9. Hunger   ....

10. Feeling of inferiority   ....

11. Success   ....

12. Malice   ....

ANSWERS: 1-weltschmerz; 2-enervation; 3-misogyny; 4-vindic-
         tiveness; 5-antipathy; 6-vicariousness; 7-ennui; 8-com-
         punction; 9-satiety; 10-superciliousness; 11-frustra-
         tion; 12-benevolence

V. Complete the following sentences by some one of the
words that are the subject of this chapter, or by some form
of that word. Not all the words may be required, and also
a given word may be asked for more than once.

1. When I reflect on the pleasant memories of my childhood, I am overcome by a wave of ....

2. Nothing I do is successful; all, all is ....

3. I would have too many .... to deprive him of
   his one chance of happiness.

4. What is life? What is to be the future of humanity?
   Shall we all finally destroy one another? I am
   weighed down with ....

5. No, I don't care to meet that beautiful actress. You
   forget that I am ....

6. No wonder you are blasé. You are suffering from a
   .... of pleasure.

7. Oh, I think I shall die if something doesn't happen to
   relieve my ....

8. You show your superiority too openly. No wonder your friends dislike you and call you ....

9. I have been unable to accomplish anything for the past two years. I seem to have sunk into a state of ....

10. .... have an .... for women.

11. You treat your employees with a pretended generosity and ...., but they see through you and know that you actually have an .... for the laboring classes.

12. Staying up with that invalid all night has reduced me to a state of ....

13. I bear you no animus for what you have done. I am not ....

14. I see the motion pictures .... even though I am blind, for my friends come home and tell me all about them.

ANSWERS: 1-nostalgia; 2-frustration; 3-compunctions; 4-weltschmerz; 5-misogynous or misogynistic; 6-satiety; 7-ennui; 8-supercilious; 9-lethargy; 10-misogynists, antipathy; 11-benevolence, antipathy; 12-enervation; 13-vindictive; 14-vicariously

---

If you breezed through this test with an average of eighty per cent or better you should be exceptionally well pleased. If most of the words were originally new to you, a mark of even fifty per cent would be creditable.

It would be a trite repetition to tell you that all of this

effort is helpful, whether or not attended by complete success. Most people, as you know, get dull as they get old. Why shouldn't we try to become more interesting; keep alert, alive? Let us be curious about things as children are. Let us plan ahead and live in the future. The mere determination to increase and improve your vocabulary will give you new horizons for old.

WORDS ABOUT PERSONALITIES

Language, most naturally, is an intensely human subject, and all words lead finally to man.

We will turn to terms that deal directly with your friends and with you. Here are twelve words that describe different kinds of personalities. They are words which describe the thoughts you have often had.

Try writing on the margin the name of some friend or relative whose personality you feel has been typified. This will bring the words to life and will fix them in your memory.

I. What kind of personality do you happen to have?

1. Are you moody, quiet, happy to be alone? Do you spend much of your time thinking of yourself? You are probably an *introvert* (in'-tro-vert).

2. Are you a good mixer? Do you prefer the company of others to solitude? Are you rarely self-conscious and usually more interested in the outside world and in the other fellow than you are in yourself? Would you be apt to make a good salesman? You are probably an *extrovert* (ex'-tro-vert).

3. Do you feel that you have some of the qualities listed in (1) combined with some of those listed in (2)? In com-

mon with most people, few of whom are *pure* introverts or extroverts, you are most likely an *ambivert* (am'-bi-vert).

4. Is your mind so selfishly occupied with your own thoughts, desires, opinions, and needs, as to make you indifferent to the interests of other folk? You are *egocentric* (egg-o-sen'-trik).

5. Do you often wish to do perfectly innocent things which your Puritan conscience, or your fear of ridicule, or your conservative upbringing, prevents you from doing? You are *inhibited* (in-hib'-i-ted).

6. Are you so completely lacking in modesty and self-consciousness that you delight in making a spectacle of yourself? Do you make a play for the spotlight and are you eager to put on a one-man show at every gathering? You are an *exhibitionist* (ex-i-bish'-un-ist).

7. Do you always think of that witty remark *after* you get home? Do you feel that your opinions are not worth expressing? Are you so completely lacking in self-confidence that you rarely achieve the success or recognition that your talents and ability seem to deserve? You are *diffident* (dif'-i-dent).

8. Are you generally gay, happy, bubbling over with zest and high spirits? You are *effervescent* (ef-er-vess'-ent).

9. Are you happiest when you are with a crowd? Do you prefer people to solitude and do you feel emotionally most content in the company of friends? You are *gregarious* (gre-gair'-ee-us).

10. Do you walk around with a chip on your shoulder? Are you always ready to do battle? Are you savage, fierce, ruthless, unyielding in your manner and in your arguments? You are *truculent* (truck'-yoo-lent).

11. Are you grave, gloomy, heavy, foreboding? Do you rarely smile? You are *saturnine* (sat'-ur-nine).

12. Are you chivalrous, romantic and idealistic almost to a ridiculous extreme? Are you the opposite of practical? Do you place woman on so high a pedestal that she is unapproachable? Are you always chasing rainbows? You are *quixotic* (kwix-ot'-ik).

II. Practice the pronunciation of such of these words as are unfamiliar to you.

1. introvert	5. inhibited	9. gregarious
2. extrovert	6. exhibitionist	10. truculent
3. ambivert	7. diffident	11. saturnine
4. egocentric	8. effervescent	12. quixotic

III. Now try the pronunciation of these forms:

1. introversion (in-tro-ver'-shun)
2. extroversion (ex-tro-ver'-shun)
3. ambiversion (am-bi-ver'-shun)
4. egocentrism (egg-o-sen'-trizm)
5. inhibition (in-hi-bish'-un)
6. exhibitionism (ex-i-bish'-un-izm)
7. diffidence (dif'-i-dence)
8. effervescence (ef-er-vess'-ence)

   9. gregariousness (gre-gair´-ee-us-ness)
  10. truculence (truck´-yoo-lence)
  11. quixoticism (kwix-ot´-i-sizm)
  12. saturninity (sa-ter-nin´-i-tee)

IV. Can you fit the above twelve words in their proper places, each to the correct definition?

   1. Possessed with self-distrust; shy; timid   ....

   2. Giving off bubbles in liquids; spar-
      kling in persons   ....

   3. Looking at everything from a personal
      point of view   ....

   4. A love of putting on an act in front of
      others   ....

   5. One whose chief interests are outside
      of himself and who makes friends
      easily   ....

   6. Habitually living or moving in com-
      pany with others, or wishing to   ....

   7. One whose interest is directed inward,
      who is turned in upon himself and
      who is much alone   ....

   8. Idealistic but impractical   ....

   9. Morose, gloomy, heavy, dull   ....

  10. Of savage character, awakening terror   ....

  11. Finding his satisfactions both within
      himself and in the outside world   ....

  12. Not able to let his hair down and have

fun because of his conscience and
early training ....

ANSWERS: 1-diffident; 2-effervescent; 3-egocentric; 4-exhibition-
ism; 5-extrovert; 6-gregarious; 7-introvert; 8-quixotic;
9-saturnine; 10-truculent; 11-ambivert; 12-inhibited

V. Write each of the above words next to its synonym or
synonymous phrase.

1. Cruel, ferocious ....
2. Shy and timid ....
3. Bubbling over ....
4. Considering self the center of everything ....
5. Psychically and mentally restrained ....
6. Loves to be the center of attention ....
7. His interests are centered in the ex-
   ternal ....
8. Liking to be with other people ....
9. His interest is directed inward ....
10. Idealistic but impractical ....
11. Gloomy and morose ....
12. He finds his satisfactions both inside
    and outside himself ....

ANSWERS: 1-truculent; 2-diffident; 3-effervescent; 4-egocentric;
5-inhibited; 6-exhibitionist; 7-extrovert; 8-gregarious;
9-introvert; 10-quixotic; 11-saturnine; 12-ambivert

With each chapter your power over words is growing. And yet it is only fair to bear in mind that you are doing much more than merely learning lists of words. In addition and in proportion to the new words that you may have learned, you must have also opened up new avenues of thought. That is what an improved vocabulary inevitably leads to. It is no accident that successful and intelligent people have the largest vocabularies. Their competence with words is a token of their success and intelligence.

ADJECTIVES GIVE YOU POWER

A vocabulary of power gives you the ability to condense a highly involved thought into a single word. Thus, if you wish to describe an action that is so ordinary and undistinguished and common that it immediately marks its perpetrator as a person completely lacking in imagination (notice how many words we have used to express this thought), you will use the word *plebeian*. On the other hand, an act that indicates excessive desire to be over-attentive, with attendant evidences of insincerity and a suspicion of ulterior motives, might be characterized as *obsequious*. Again, an action that is sickeningly sentimental and indicative of emotional immaturity, and one that is often accompanied by tears, could be called *maudlin*.

I. There are many such words that compress a wealth of meaning and emotion into a few syllables. Note how expressive the following phrases are:

 1. A *plebeian* (ple-bee'-an) outlook on life
 2. *Obsequious* (ob-se'-kwee-us) attentions of the head-waiter
 3. A *maudlin* (maud'-lin) motion picture

4. A *perfunctory* (per-funk'-toe-ree) examination by the inefficient doctor

5. An *abortive* (a-bor'-tiv) attempt to gain his ends

6. A *surreptitious* (sur-rep-tish'-us) movement on the part of the thief

7. A *presumptuous* (pre-zump'-choo-us) question to put to royalty

8. The *sadistic* (sa-dis'-tik) treatment of the prisoner

9. A *flagrant* (flay'-grant) misuse of company funds

10. An *inane* (in-ayn') remark

From an analysis of these phrases, write the proper word next to its definition.

1. Openly scandalous; notorious; heinous ....

2. Senseless; silly; empty ....

3. Made foolish by liquor; tearfully affectionate ....

4. Cringing and servile in manner ....

5. Done mechanically and without interest; superficial and careless ....

6. Unduly confident or bold; audacious; arrogant; insolent ....

7. Inclined to cruelty; getting pleasure out of hurting others ....

8. Accomplishment by secret or improper
   means   ....

9. Common; inferior   ....

10. Coming to naught; failing   ....

ANSWERS: 1-flagrant; 2-inane; 3-maudlin; 4-obsequious; 5-per-
         functory; 6-presumptuous; 7-sadistic; 8-surreptitious;
         9-plebeian; 10-abortive

───────────

II. And to this we will add another list of valuable and
    much used words.

   1. *Wanton* (wahn'-ton) cruelty

   2. *Crass* (crass) behavior

   3. *Macabre* (ma-kah'-ber) mystery

   4. *Dogmatic* (dog-mat'-ik) assertion

   5. *Vitriolic* (vit-ree-ol'-ik) satire

   6. *Intermittent* (in-ter-mit'-ent) ringing of the tele-
      phone

   7. *Subversive* (sub-ver'-siv) activities of the com-
      munists

   8. *Desultory* (dess'-ul-toe-ree) flitting from one sub-
      ject to another

   9. A *sardonic* (sar-don'-ik) smile

Once more please write each of the preceding words opposite the proper definition below.

1. Passing irregularly from one thing to another; changeable; without method.   ....

2. Marked by positive or authoritative assertion.   ....

3. This word has two rather different meanings. It may mean lewd, lascivious, lustful when used to describe a person, usually a woman. However, when applied to an act it means recklessly inconsiderate or heartless; unrestrained; extravagant.   ....

4. Coarse in structure; heavy; dull.   ....

5. To cease and start again; to proceed at intervals; to recur, as "an .... pain."   ....

6. Insincere and derisive; sneering.   ....

7. Pertaining to, indicative of, or suggesting death, as in: "That was a .... dance."   ....

8. Corrosive; burning; caustic.   ....

9. Tending to overthrow from the very foundations, as of a moral or political force; used as in: "His remarks were .... to the welfare of the nation."   ....

ANSWERS: 1-desultory; 2-dogmatic; 3-wanton; 4-crass; 5-intermittent; 6-sardonic; 7-macabre; 8-vitriolic; 9-subversive

III. Can you change each of these adjectives to some other part of speech? Then try changing:

1. *Obsequious* to a noun: "His .... was annoying."

2. *Perfunctory* to an adverb: "He did his work ...."

3. *Surreptitious* to an adverb: "He crept through the house ...."

4. *Presumptuous* to a noun: "Your .... will be punished."

5. *Sadistic* to a noun denoting the person: "He is a ...."

6. *Sadistic* to a noun denoting the philosophy: "He practices ...."

7. *Flagrant* to a noun: "I cannot understand how you can break the law with such ...."

8. *Inane* to a plural noun: "His speech is full of ...."

9. *Wanton* to an adverb: "...................., she broke her suitors' hearts."

10. *Crass* to a noun: "His .... makes it impossible for him to be accepted by refined people."

11. *Dogmatic* to a noun: "Why do you always speak with such ....?"

12. *Intermittent* to an adverb: "The rain came down ...."

13. *Desultory* to an adverb: "He reads ...."

ANSWERS: 1-obsequiousness; 2-perfunctorily; 3-surreptitiously;
4-presumption; 5-sadist; 6-sadism; 7-flagrancy; 8-inani-
ties; 9-wantonly; 10-crassness; 11-dogmatism; 12-in-
termittently; 13-desultorily

———————

IV. After studying the words carefully, complete the following sentences with the word that you think comes
nearest to the general meaning. This is not a test of
accuracy, but is more in the nature of a five-finger
exercise.

1. He made an (a).............. attempt to regain the
governorship; his defeat left him a sad and bitter
man who thereafter looked on life bitterly and
....

2. Can you think of anything quite so .... cruel
as war?

3. Pompous people delight in .... attendance
on their every wish.

4. Thievery will out, and anything you do ....
will some day come back to haunt you.

5. Please don't state so .... that Democracy is
a fiasco. Time will show the stupidity of such a
statement.

6. It was easy to see that he disliked his job heartily
and therefore it was no surprise that he discharged
his duties so ....

7. With what malicious and .... satisfaction
the prosecutor made the witness reveal his past!

8. Read with a purpose; .... reading is neither satisfactory nor sensible.

9. No one can deny that the dictators have made .... attacks on their opponents.

10. Economic recovery seems to be ....; now you see it, now you don't.

11. His crime was so glaring and .... that everyone knew about it.

12. Isn't it rather .... for a person of your reputation to ask to be my friend?

13. During election times, candidates make such .... attacks on the characters of their opponents that their remarks burn and sear.

14. The .... destruction of life and property in wartime is perhaps the strongest argument against war.

15. He made a futile and .... attempt at rescue.

16. Such .... and gross materialism will never lead to real happiness.

ANSWERS: 1-abortive, sardonically; 2-wantonly; 3-obsequious; 4-surreptitiously; 5-dogmatically; 6-perfunctorily; 7-sadistic; 8-desultory; 9-flagrant, inane, wanton, crass, or vitriolic; 10-intermittent; 11-flagrant; 12-presumptuous; 13-vitriolic; 14-wanton; 15-abortive; 16-crass

---

The answers given above are not necessarily the only possible ones. In some of the sentences several of the words will fit. As a person whose vocabulary is becoming daily larger and larger you will easily realize that there are a multitude of ways of saying the same thing. But the particular word you choose will determine the flavor of your thought. This is the priceless value of a large vocabulary. Out of your wide range of words you can then pick the particular one that will best express each subtle nuance of your mind.

LEARNING WORDS THE MODERN WAY

This book is not a memory course.

Merely memorizing lists of words by rote happens to be the slowest and most difficult way to remember them. If you follow such a routine you will find that you have forgotten most of the list by the next day.

What, then, is the correct procedure?

Just this.

Look at the word first, if you can, in its context: in the paragraph where it appears. The very sense of the paragraph will give you an inkling of the significance of the word—even if you have never seen it before. You naturally become eager to know the definition of the word in order to understand the sentence pattern in which you have seen it: Your approach, then, is *indirect and psychological,* because you wish the information, not as an end in itself, but as a means to an end. You realize that if you learn the meaning of the word you will comprehend the meaning of the sentence. You are using what is called the modern *inductive* method, in that you first discover the word at work, you are challenged by it, you guess at its meaning, and you then confirm or correct your guess by referring to the dictionary.

When you use this method, the words are no longer so much dead wood, to be piled up in your mind, but are living entities, charged with action and emotion. They then become hard to forget.

Let's be specific and illustrate our point.

We will discuss thirteen adverbs and two adverbial phrases and try to prove how much easier it is to learn by the *indirect, inductive and psychological* route.

I. Give your careful attention to the following sentences in Groups A, B, C, D and E. In each sentence you will find an adverb in italics. If the word is new to you try to guess at its meaning and keep it in mind. You are going to be asked about it.

Group A

1. He complained *acrimoniously* (ack-ri-mo'-nee-us-lee).
2. We argued *acrimoniously*.
3. They mocked each other *acrimoniously*.

   (You can feel the unpleasant overtone of this word, can't you?)

Group B

1. He completed the operation *adroitly* (a-droyt'-lee).
2. He drove *adroitly* through the maze of traffic.
3. *Adroitly* she knitted the complicated stitch.

   (This word obviously applies to some manual action.)

Group C

1. He moved slowly and *circumspectly* (sir'-cum-spec-lee) through the range of fire.

2. Fearing a trick, he answered all questions *circumspectly*.
3. By walking *circumspectly* he avoided an ambush.

   (There's a feeling of watchfulness about this word.)

Group D

1. These two building leases run *concomitantly* (con-com'-i-tant-lee).
2. Living and learning go on *concomitantly*.
3. Rain, snow, and sleet, all came down *concomitantly*.

   (You probably know why two or more things must be involved in these actions, even if you happen never to have seen the word before.)

Group E

1. He examined the plans *cursorily* (cur'-so-ri-lee).
2. He ran through the pages *cursorily,* then threw the novel down in disgust.
3. He did his homework so *cursorily* that he flunked his examination.

   (This word should carry an impression of superficial haste.)

Remember your ideas of these meanings and of the meanings of the words in italics in Sections II and III as you are going to have a test on them in Section IV.

II. Now you are ready to tackle five more words. Examine (but not cursorily!) the following statements and come as close as possible to figuring out the meanings of those that are new to you.

1. Teachers are apt to talk *didactically* (dye-dack´-tik-a-lee).

2. Extremely modest persons usually speak of their own accomplishments *disparagingly* (dis-par´-a-jing-lee).

3. People with extremely facile and ready tongues can talk *glibly* (glib´-lee).

4. The person who is looking for sympathy talks *plaintively* (plain´-tiv-lee).

5. Pessimists usually speak *ominously* (om´-i-nus-lee) of the future.

III. Are any of the following words strange to you? If so please guess at their meanings as best you can.

1. Man cannot break the laws of nature with *impunity* (im-pyoo´-ni-tee).

2. He placed his hand on the hot radiator *inadvertently* (in-ad-vert´-ent-lee).

3. He was a disagreeable old man who answered every question *irascibly* (eye-rass´-ib-lee).

4. Inasmuch as the plans were executed *sub rosa* (sub ro´-za) the stockholders realized too late how completely they had been mulcted.

5. He never gave up quietly. He always complained *vociferously* (vo-sif´-er-us-lee) if he thought he had been treated unfairly.

IV. Now see if you can write each of the words that you have had in Sections I, II and III in its correct place opposite what you believe to be its correct meaning in the list below.

1. Expertly; dexterously; with skillful use of the hands or mind ....

2. Accompanying; occurring together ....

3. In the fashion of a teacher; as if teaching a lesson ....

4. In a manner of smooth ease and fluency; without hesitation ....

5. In a heedless manner; without care; inattentively ....

6. Forebodingly; in a way portending evil ....

7. In strict confidence; privately ....

8. In a loud-voiced manner; vehemently; noisily ....

9. Expressing sadness or melancholy ....

10. Angrily; irritably; in hot-tempered fashion ....

11. With freedom from punishment or injurious consequences ....

12. Speaking slightingly of, in a way to undervalue and discredit ....

13. Doing something hastily and superficially without due care and attention ....

14. Cautiously with watchfulness in all directions ....

15. With sharpness and bitterness of speech or temper ....

ANSWERS: (Also serving to explain the sentences in Groups A, B, C, D and E and in Sections II and III): 1-adroitly; 2-concomitantly; 3-didactically; 4-glibly; 5-inadvertently; 6-ominously; 7-sub rosa; 8-vociferously; 9-plaintively; 10-irascibly; 11-with impunity; 12-disparagingly; 13-cursorily; 14-circumspectly; 15-acrimoniously

———

V. The following drill will be well worth your effort. We will give you 46 synonyms or synonymous phrases that are descriptive of the thirteen adverbs and two adverbial phrases you have just had. That is, each adverb will have to be written in several times opposite the words that you think come nearest to its meaning. If you make some mistakes don't be in the least discouraged. The whole object of this device is to help clinch the meanings of these words in your mind.

1. hastily	....	11. dexterously	....
2. warily	....	12. cautiously	....
3. teacher-like	....	13. slightingly	....
4. cholerically	....	14. easily	....
5. in a way fore-boding evil	....	15. caustically	....
6. sadly	....	16. heedlessly	....
7. covertly	....	17. at the same time	....
8. loudly	....	18. angrily	....
9. inauspiciously	....	19. prudently	....
10. testily	....		

20. with exemp-
tion from pun-
ishment ....

21. smoothly ....

22. stingingly ....

23. thoughtlessly ....

24. deprecatingly ....

25. conjointly ....

26. without harm ....

27. bitterly ....

28. fluently ....

29. depreciatively ....

30. ingeniously ....

31. irately ....

32. portentously ....

33. sorrowfully ....

34. without pun-
ishment ....

35. rapidly ....

36. like an in-
structor ....

37. mournfully ....

38. privately ....

39. clamorously ....

40. blatantly ....

41. noisily ....

42. instructively ....

43. confidentially ....

44. in a melan-
choly way ....

45. belittlingly ....

46. superficially ....

ANSWERS: 1-cursorily; 2-circumspectly; 3-didactically; 4-irasci-
bly; 5-ominously; 6-plaintively; 7-sub rosa; 8-vocif-
erously; 9-ominously; 10-irascibly; 11-adroitly; 12-
circumspectly; 13-disparagingly; 14-glibly; 15-acri-
moniously; 16-inadvertently; 17-concomitantly; 18-
irascibly; 19-circumspectly; 20-with impunity; 21-glib-
ly; 22-acrimoniously; 23-inadvertently; 24-disparag-
ingly; 25-concomitantly; 26-with impunity; 27-acri-
moniously; 28-glibly; 29-disparagingly; 30-adroitly;
31-irascibly; 32-ominously; 33-plaintively; 34-with
impunity; 35-cursorily; 36-didactically; 37-plaintively;
38-sub rosa; 39-vociferously; 40-vociferously; 41-vocif-
erously; 42-didactically; 43-sub rosa; 44-plaintively;
45-disparagingly; 46-cursorily

VI. Choose and write in the spaces below, seven of the adverbs or adverbial phrases you have been studying that you think will best fit the seven situations portrayed below.

1. You are a burglar. You have just entered a wealthy home through an unlocked window. All is dark, and alas, you have forgotten to bring your searchlight with you. To add to your troubles, you can't find the electric switch. How will you move around in this room until you can get your bearings?   ....

2. You are an irritable, touchy old man, and as you walk along the street on this cold, raw morning you feel nothing but enmity toward the whole world. A beggar stops you for a coin. How do you refuse? ....

3. A friend has been importuning you for weeks to look over a novel he is writing and give him your criticism. Knowing your friend you are certain that the novel is bad even before you read it; besides you are a very busy man. Rather than give your friend a blunt refusal, however, you take the manuscript home one evening. How do you examine it?   ....

4. Your small son wishes to know why it snows. You are well versed in the natural sciences and have made it a habit to answer all your son's questions as clearly and accurately as possible. How do you answer him?

    ....

5. You have influence with the chief of police and, furthermore, your wife is the mayor's daughter. Consequently, you never trouble to obey traffic laws. In fact, you can break them.   ....

6. A woman has broken your heart purposely, and with malice aforethought. She has left you a disillusioned man. It takes you years even to begin to get over it. And then one day you meet her again. She is gay, debonair; she has obviously forgotten what she has done to you. This angers you and you intend to sting her when you remind her of what she has done to you. In what fashion do you speak to her? ....

7. You are a very modest person. Rather than praise anything you have done, you prefer to take as little credit as possible for your accomplishments. How do you usually speak of yourself? ....

ANSWERS: 1-circumspectly; 2-irascibly; 3-cursorily; 4-didactically; 5-with impunity; 6-acrimoniously; 7-disparagingly

———————

VII. One of the quickest ways of improving and increasing your vocabulary is to practice turning words into other forms. Can you change the adverbs in this chapter into their noun forms?

1. acrimoniously ....   8. glibly   ....
2. adroitly   ....   9. plaintively   ....
3. circumspectly ....   10. ominously   ....
4. concomitantly ....   11. inadvertently   ....
5. cursorily   ....   12. irascibly   ....
6. didactically   ....   13. vociferously   ....
7. disparagingly ....

ANSWERS: 1-acrimony; 2-adroitness; 3-circumspection; 4-con-
comitance; 5-cursoriness; 6-didacticism; 7-disparage-
ment; 8-glibness; 9-plaintiveness; 10-ominousness;
11-inadvertence; 12-irascibility; 13-vociferousness

———————

Occasionally you may feel that these exercises are time-
consuming. But we urge you never to let the lack of time
stand as an obstacle to your work. Thomas Carlyle, the
great philosopher, claimed that there is time in every man's
life for a career within a career. Even so-called geniuses
are largely geniuses because they are willing to use the
time that others throw away. It was Michelangelo who
said: "If people only knew how hard I work to gain my
mastery it wouldn't seem so wonderful at all." And Alex-
andre Dumas, the prolific French novelist, confessed:
"Infatuated, half through conceit, half through love of my
art, I achieve the impossible working as none else ever
works. . . ."

Careers are not had by wishing and hoping. They are
bought with work and enthusiasm.

WORDS FROM THE LATIN

A large part of our English vocabulary, as we know, derives from the Latin. This language is no longer used in the living sense except in the somewhat modified form of what is known as "Church Latin." Old Latin was no longer a spoken tongue when modern English began, yet English is such a vital and avid tongue that it has steadily fed upon Latin, and even today this Roman speech is being constantly taken over into English by scholars, philologists and scientists.

Any time you run an inquisitive plow through our language you turn up Latin roots everywhere.

I. There is the simple word "animal." Why particularly do we use the word "animal" instead of some other combination of syllables?

"Animal" is from the Latin word, *anima,* meaning "breath," "soul," or "spirit," and, of course, animals, as opposed to minerals or "inanimate" objects, do breathe and do possess that mysterious something that gives to them a life not found in "inanimate" things. The stem of *anim* is found in a host of common English words:

*anim*alcule—A tiny live thing
*anim*ate—To breathe life into

equa*nim*ity—Equal or placid spirit or mind

magn*anim*ous—Of large, or noble spirit

un*anim*ous—Of one mind

in*anim*ate—Without a soul; not alive

*anim*osity—Vehement enmity

pusill*anim*ous—Faint-hearted; cowardly

*anim*advert—To turn the mind to; to notice; to criticize

II. In many cases, English words are formed by combining parts of two or more Latin words. Thus "equanimity" is a fusion of *aequus,* "equal," and *anima.* You will recognize this new stem in such words as "equation," "equality," "equity," "iniquity." "Magnanimous" combines *magnus,* "large" with *anima.* Engage in a little etymological exploration, if you will, and see what other words you can turn up with the stem of *magnus,* "large."

1.	A person large in importance, as in an industry
2.	To make large
3.	Splendor; grandeur
4.	Speaking big or in pompous or flowery style
5.	Bigness or greatness
6.	A large bottle (2 quarts) for champagne or other wine
7.	A great work; a literary or artistic work of importance

ANSWERS: 1-magnate; 2-magnify; 3-magnificence; 4-magnilo-
quent; 5-magnitude; 6-magnum; 7-magnum opus

III. "Unanimous" combines *unus,* "one," with *anima,*
"mind." Can you think of some other English words
which contain the stem of *unus*?

1. .... Make into one

2. .... A fabulous animal with a single,
straight horn

3. .... Of one form or kind

4. .... The state of being united

5. .... The only one of its kind

6. .... Harmony; also a joining together

ANSWERS: 1-unify or unite; 2-unicorn; 3-uniform; 4-union; 5-
unique; 6-unison

IV. Continuing our etymological exploration, let us next
consider the word *benevolence.* Its meaning—"a feeling
of good will towards others" or "charitable action for the
benefit of others"—can be understood better when we
analyze the two Latin roots that have been welded together to form the word: *bene,* "well" and *volens* "wishing." Benevolence means, literally, "wishing others well."
Bene is found in other words. Here are a few:

*bene*fit   *bene*ficiary   *bene*diction   *bene*factor

The stem of *volens*, "wishing," also appears frequently:

*vol*ition   *vol*untary   *vol*unteer

If we now dissect two of the words containing *bene*, we will discover that new Latin stems can easily be added to our repertoire: *benediction*, "a blessing," is, literally, a "saying well." The stem *dic* is from the Latin *dicere*, meaning "to say" or "to tell." You can see it in the following words:

*dic*tate   *dic*taphone   *dic*tion   male*dic*tion
              in*dict*   pre*dict*

Again, "benefactor," literally "well-doer," contains *fac* (from the Latin verb *facere*) meaning "to do" or "to make." Watch how this stem is employed in the following words:

*fac*tor   *fac*tory   manu*fac*ture   *fact*   *fac*totum   *fac*tual

Thus, the study of a few of these simple words brings to light eight new stems. Here are the Latin words with their meanings and with the part that serves as a stem in italics. Can you think up an English word using each stem and write it in below?

Stem	Meaning	Example
1. *anim*a	soul, spirit, mind	....
2. *aequ*us	even, equal	....

3. *magn*us — large, big, great ....

4. *un*us — one, single ....

5. *bene* — well ....

6. *vol*ens — wishing ....

7. *fac*ere — to do, to make ....

8. *dic*ere — to say, to tell ....

And now can you recall to your memory the other Greek and Latin stems that you have had in this book? In the chart below you will find a list of them, each with an example. Can you fill in the English meaning of each stem, starting with *mono*?

1. mono (monocle) ....

2. bi (bicycle) ....

3. poly (polygamy) ....

4. miso (misogyny) ....

5. gamy (bigamy) ....

6. theo (monotheism) ....

7. anthropo (anthropology) ....

8. philo (philatelist) ....

9. logy (philology) ....

ANSWERS: 1-one; 2-two; 3-many; 4-hatred of; 5-marriage; 6-God; 7-man; 8-love of; 9-knowledge, study of

You will find it excellent practice to keep a weather eye out for these roots and for their various and varied combinations in your daily reading There are so many of them, that it becomes a fascinating sport to try to trace, them. There is the Latin word *signa,* or "sign," which give us in*sign*ia, the *sign* you wear; *sign*al, a sign; *sign*ify, make a sign; and such others as de*sign, sign*ature, in*sign*ificant. We also have the Latin term *portare,* "to carry," which leads to *port*er, one who carries; *port*able, able to be carried; re*port*er, one who carries news back; de*port,* carry away; im*port,* carry in; and ex*port,* carry out.

A knowledge of Latin and Greek roots is a splendid little vocabulary stretcher.

TEST YOUR PROGRESS

There is one thing that we cannot over-emphasize in this daily word study, and that is the high importance of continually reviewing the work that you have done. New words that come into your vocabulary are as elusive as little shining eels, and unless you rehearse them constantly you will find that they will wriggle out from between your mental fingers and slip back into the sea of language.

If you want to make swift progress, take each page of this book seriously, review your work as a matter of course, and so make good the ground as you proceed.

Here is another hint. Be sure to finish this book. Forty-nine out of fifty persons don't thoroughly finish what they begin. This is what will make success so easy for you. Use your will power. Will power is often just another name for courage. Perseverance is energy made habitual. And perseverance, continuously applied, may become genius. So don't just finish this book—or this chapter—and lay it aside. Put it to work. Too many people are forever learning and never doing.

Right now we are going to challenge you with a partial review of Chapters 10 to 21. This review will not be an easy one, but whether you fail or succeed, it will help to show up any weak spots in your methods of study.

I. Below we give you two lists, A and B. Under "A" are ten words that you have had. Under "B" are short descriptions of the words. Run down "B" and first pick the description that best fits "atheist" and write down the identifying letter. That is, if an "atheist" is a "loud-mouthed woman" (which it isn't) you would mark "a" after "atheist."

Please don't look up the answers that are given at the end of this chapter until you are completely through with the ten tests. Take off one point for each error.

A.	B.
1. atheist	a. Loud-mouthed woman
2. virtuoso	b. Connoisseur of good food
3. virago	c. Disbeliever in God
4. gourmet	d. Beginner
5. tyro	e. One who leads a severe life
6. philatelist	f. Stamp collector
7. ascetic	g. Traitor
8. pedant	h. Bootlicker
9. judas	i. Skilled practitioner of the arts
10. sycophant	j. One who is ostentatious about his learning

II. The following phrases give a brief description of the mental diseases and phobias you read about in Chapter 11. Can you identify them and complete the words whose initial letters are given?

1. Insane desire to set fires   P ....

2. Uncontrollable propensity to steal   K ....

3. Forgetfulness of the past   A ....

4. Sleep-walking   S ....

5. Alternating fits of despondency and hilarity   M ....

6. Split personality   S ....

7. Fear of closed spaces   C ....

8. Continuous drunkenness   D ....

9. Persecution complex   P ....

10. Fear of large spaces   A ....

III. Examine the fifteen words in group A and write each one in the space allowed for it, opposite its proper identifying word or phrase in group B.

A lethargy   weltschmerz   superciliousness

    nostalgia   antipathy   vindictiveness

    benevolence   compunction   misogyny

    satiety   enervation   misanthropy

    frustration   ennui   vicariousness

B 1. Homesickness ....

    2. Good will to all ....

    3. Repletion ....

    4. Thwarting ....

    5. Dislike ....

6. World-sorrow ....

7. Hatred of women ....

8. Scruple ....

9. Revengefulness ....

10. Haughtiness ....

11. Sluggishness ....

12. Exhaustion ....

13. Boredom ....

14. Hatred of mankind ....

15. Indirect experience ....

IV. Name and write in the science which deals with each of the following subjects. The initial letter of the correct word is given.

1. Mankind	A....................logy	
2. Rocks	G....................logy	
3. Ancient relics	A....................logy	
4. Unborn babies	E....................logy	
5. Insects	E....................logy	
6. Distribution of races	E....................logy	
7. Derivation of words	E....................logy	
8. Birds	O....................logy	
9. Languages	P....................logy	
10. The human mind	P....................logy	

V. Here are two columns of ten words each. Where the words opposite each other are synonyms, write the letter "S" next to the pair. Where they have opposite meanings, write "O." Where the words have no relationship to each other, write "N."

1. loquacious	....	talkative
2. gullible	....	shrewd
3. suave	....	happy
4. pompous	....	conceited
5. taciturn	....	silent
6. phlegmatic	....	excitable
7. erudite	....	ignorant
8. complacent	....	constant
9. punctilious	....	careless
10. indefatigable	....	tireless

VI. In column A are ten definitions; in column B are ten blanks, each with an initial and final letter. The definitions in column A and the words to be supplied in column B do not necessarily face each other. It is up to you to unscramble the columns and fill in the remaining letters of each word. For instance, start with #1, "minor indiscretion." Now run down column B and see if (with the initial and last letters to guide you) you can recall the word that the phrase "minor indiscretion" describes. When you succeed in remembering it, fill it in.

A.	B.
1. minor indiscretion	1. P .... y
2. poverty	2. M .... r
3. boastfulness	3. J .... m
4. cure-all	4. B .... o
5. failure	5. P .... a
6. characteristic peculiarity	6. P .... o
7. irregularity	7. F .... o
8. war-mongering	8. A .... y
9. pretend illness	9. C .... y
10. trickery	10. I .... y

VII. Fit each word in column B to its proper defining word or phrase in column A. Write one of the letters, *a* to *j*, opposite the proper definition in column A.

A.	B.
1. one whose mind is turned inward	a. diffident
2. self-centered	b. extrovert
3. restrained	c. inhibited
4. modest	d. saturnine
5. bubbling over with high spirits	e. egocentric
6. company loving	f. quixotic
7. fierce; overbearing	g. introvert
8. gloomy	h. effervescent
9. extravagantly chivalrous	i. truculent
10. one whose mind is turned outward	j. gregarious

VIII. In each of the five lines below there is one word that correctly expresses the meaning given in the word or words in italics just ahead. Check either a, b or c, whichever one may be correct.

1. *common, ordinary:* a. plebeian, b. obsequious, c. maudlin

2. *miserably failing:* a. perfunctory, b. abortive, c. surreptitious

3. *cruel:* a. presumptuous, b. sadistic, c. flagrant

4. *vulgar:* a. inane, b. wanton, c. crass

5. *biting:* a. macabre, b. dogmatic, c. vitriolic

IX. Proceed as in Test VIII.

1. *at the same time:* a. acrimoniously, b. adroitly, c. concomitantly

2. *carefully:* a. circumspectly, b. cursorily, c. didactically

3. *smoothly:* a. disparagingly, b. glibly, c. plaintively

4. *threateningly:* a. ominously, b. with impunity, c. inadvertently

5. *secretly:* a. irascibly, b. sub rosa, c. vociferously

X. Write the English meaning of each italicized Greek or Latin stem in the blank space opposite.

1. *magn*animous ....

2. *uni*que ....

3. un*anim*ous ....

4. *bene*fit ....

5. bene*vol*ence ....

6. *dic*taphone ....

7. manu*fac*ture ....

8. mono*gamy* ....

9. *theo*logy ....

10. *bi*cycle ....

ANSWERS:

I.   1-c; 2-i; 3-a; 4-b; 5-d; 6-f; 7-e; 8-j; 9-g; 10-h

II. 1-pyromania; 2-kleptomania; 3-amnesia; 4-somnambulism; 5-manic-depression; 6-schizophrenia; 7-claustrophobia; 8-dipsomania; 9-paranoia; 10-agoraphobia

III. 1-nostalgia; 2-benevolence; 3-satiety; 4-frustration; 5-antipathy; 6-weltschmerz; 7-misogyny; 8-compunction; 9-vindictiveness; 10-superciliousness; 11-lethargy; 12-enervation; 13-ennui; 14-misanthropy; 15-vicariousness

IV. 1-anthropology; 2-geology; 3-archaeology; 4-embryology; 5-entomology; 6-ethnology; 7-etymology; 8-ornithology; 9-philology; 10-psychology

V.   1-s; 2-o; 3-n; 4-s; 5-s; 6-o; 7-o; 8-n; 9-o; 10-s

VI. 1-peccadillo; 2-penury; 3-braggadocio; 4-panacea; 5-fiasco; 6-idiosyncrasy; 7-anomaly; 8-jingoism; 9-malinger; 10-chicanery

VII. 1-g; 2-e; 3-c; 4-a; 5-h; 6-j; 7-i; 8-d; 9-f; 10-b

VIII. 1-a; 2-b; 3-b; 4-c; 5-c

IX. 1-c; 2-a; 3-b; 4-a; 5-b

X.   1-large; 2-one; 3-mind or spirit; 4-well; 5-wish; 6-say; 7-make; 8-marriage; 9-God; 10-two

In case you feel that you should refer again to the lessons that have been covered in these tests, let us give you the order. Section I in this present chapter is a review of Chapter 10; Section II of Chapter 11; III of 12; IV of 13; V of 14; VI of 15; VII of 18; VIII of 19; IX of 20; X of 21.

In rating yourself on the tests you have just completed 95 would be perfect. You can consider 65 as a very creditable passing mark; 80 or above would be unusually excellent. Below 50 indicates the need for better study methods.

If your score isn't as creditable as you would like, don't feel the least bit discouraged. And whatever your age, don't use the excuse that "you can't teach an old dog new tricks."

This ancient belief has been entirely disproved by an exhaustive series of tests conducted under the direction of Dr. Irving Lorge, a psychologist, while he was at Columbia University. He established the fact that the human mind retains its full powers up to the most advanced age. The *speed* of thinking is usually a little less, but *without exception* the power element shows no decline whatsoever with people even up to 90 years of age.

So Dr. Lorge has deprived us of the easy and comfortable alibi of age!

CAN YOU MEET THIS CHALLENGE?

Continuing our *inductive, psychological,* and *indirect* method of building vocabulary, which we discussed in Chapter 20, we shall now throw you pell-mell into a quiz to test your understanding of a group of words before going on to consider them. In each of the fifteen sentences that follow you will find one or two words in italics. If the words are strange to you, read the sentence carefully. Then, in each case, put a check after the particular phrase—either a, b or c—which you think comes nearest the meaning.

I.—1. If spelling is your *bête noire* (bet nwahr)
    a. You love spelling
    b. You are a good speller
    c. You hate spelling

  2. If your friend looked *cadaverous* (ca-dav'-er-us) you would say to him:
    a. When did you get up from sleep?
    b. Better stop eating so many sweets.
    c. What cemetery do you live in?

3. If the President wants *carte blanche* (cart blahnsh) in allocating defense funds
   a. He wishes no strings to be attached to the money
   b. He does not want special funds earmarked
   c. He wants instructions from Congress on how to spend it

4. *Esoteric* (ess-o-ter'-ik) knowledge is
   a. Knowledge possessed by a few
   b. Useless knowledge
   c. Knowledge that was buried with the fall of ancient civilization

5. The man who says that psychology is his *forte* (fort) means
   a. He hates the subject
   b. He's particularly good in the subject
   c. He loves the subject

6. When you come to an *impasse* (im'-pass)
   a. Stop, look and listen!
   b. You find yourself completely blocked in a certain situation
   c. Wait for a guide to show you the way out

7. *Incongruous* (in-con'-groo-us) means
   a. Out of place or character
   b. Not honest
   c. Not useful

8. *Docile* (doss'-ill) people are
   a. Stupid
   b. Lovable
   c. Easily managed

9. *Miscegenation* (miss-e-jen-ay'-shun) is marriage between
   a. A Presbyterian and an Episcopalian
   b. An heiress and a pauper
   c. A white person and a Negro

10. *Moribund* (mor'-i-bund) institutions
    a. Are passing out of existence
    b. Are in charge of dishonest people
    c. Are undemocratic

11. A *nebulous* (neb'-you-lus) ideal is one that is
    a. Heaven-sent
    b. Vague
    c. As pure as clouds

12. People who indulge in *recriminations* (ree-crim-i-nay'-shunz) are probably
    a. Playing a game
    b. Quarreling
    c. Writing letters

13. The *repercussions* (ree-per-cush'-unz) of an event must happen
    a. Before
    b. After
    c. At the same time

14. *Scurrilous* (scur'-il-us) language would more than likely be heard in
    a. The halls of Congress
    b. A quarrel between two stevedores
    c. A sermon

15. *Soporific* (so-por-if'-ik) speakers tend to
    a. Stimulate you to action

b. Appeal to your nobler instincts
c. Put you to sleep

ANSWERS: 1-c; 2-c; 3-a; 4-a; 5-b; 6-b; 7-a; 8-c; 9-c; 10-a;
11-b; 12-b; 13-b; 14-b; 15-c

II. The above words are extremely valuable to anyone, but on the whole they are quite difficult and their meanings are known to comparatively few. The following exercise will help fix the unfamiliar ones in the mind of the reader. Several of the words are repeated with different definitions. Please fill in each of the twenty blank spaces with the word that fits the definition.

1. A particular object of hate or dread ....

2. Pale; ghastly ....

3. Unconditional permission or authority ....

4. Confined to a select circle ....

5. One's strong point ....

6. Corpse-like ....

7. A blind alley; an insurmountable obstacle ....

8. For the initiated few ....

9. Inadaptable; out of place ....

10. Tractable ....

11. Dead-end ....

12. An object of dread ....

13. Marriage of mixed races ....

14. In a dying state ....

15. Hazy; indistinct ....

16. Charges retorted; abusive argument ....

17. Reverberations ....

18. Grossly offensive or vulgar ....

19. Tending to produce sleep ....

20. Pale and gaunt ....

ANSWERS: 1-bête noire; 2-cadaverous; 3-carte blanche; 4-eso-
teric; 5-forte; 6-cadaverous; 7-impasse; 8-esoteric;
9-incongruous; 10-docile; 11-impasse; 12-bête noire;
13-miscegenation; 14-moribund; 15-nebulous; 16-re-
criminations; 17-repercussions; 18-scurrilous; 19-
soporific; 20-cadaverous

———————

III. Here is another list of twenty descriptive phrases.
We have shuffled the words, and again have repeated several. Follow the same procedure as in Section II.

1. Intermarriage of races ....

2. Confined to a particular circle ....

3. Without condition ....

4. Inextricable difficulty ....

5. Incompatible ....

6. On the point of dying ....

7. Confused and hazy ....

8. Vulgar abuse ....

9. Black marries white   ....

10. Dead-end alley   ....

11. Ghastly   ....

12. Bugaboo   ....

13. Something in which one excels ....

14. Manageable   ....

15. Hazy   ....

16. Echoes   ....

17. Producing sleep   ....

18. Occidental weds Oriental   ....

19. For a few   ....

20. Specialty   ....

ANSWERS: 1-miscegenation; 2-esoteric; 3-carte blanche; 4-im-
         passe; 5-incongruous; 6-moribund; 7-nebulous; 8-
         scurrilous; 9-miscegenation; 10-impasse; 11-cadaver-
         ous; 12-bête noire; 13-forte; 14-docile; 15-nebulous;
         16-repercussions; 17-soporific; 18-miscegenation; 19-
         esoteric; 20-forte

———————

IV. Once again we will mix up a few of these words. Complete the following fifteen sentences, filling in the blank spaces with the words you have just had that best fit the meanings.

1. Some think that democracy in Europe is ....

2. Knowledge of Oriental magic is highly ....

3. Jews were Hitler's ....

4. A man suffering from consumption may look
....

5. The facts behind a politician's statements are often
....

6. What is the one thing you hate or fear most? What is
your particular ....?

7. After a dynamic presidential speech one often hears
.... abroad.

8. A party to a mixed marriage is involved in ....

9. When a husband and wife quarrel they frequently indulge in bitter ....

10. A lecturer with a monotonous voice often produces a
.... effect.

11. Angry truckdrivers frequently use .... language.

12. What are you most skilled at? What is your special
...................?

13. The cow is a very .... animal.

14. A fat and awkward girl would look .... in the
ballet.

15. An unwilling Congress no longer seems to wish to
give the President ....

ANSWERS: 1-moribund; 2-esoteric; 3-bête noire; 4-cadaverous;
5-nebulous; 6-bête noire; 7-repercussions; 8-miscege-
nation; 9-recriminations; 10-soporific; 11-scurrilous;
12-forte; 13-docile; 14-incongruous; 15-carte blanche

V. Which of the words you have been studying is exactly *opposite* in meaning to each of the following definitions? Write your answers in the blank spaces. Some words will be repeated.

1. Known to all ....

2. Caucasian marries Caucasian ....

3. In keeping with surroundings ....

4. Stimulating, like coffee ....

5. Radiantly healthy ....

6. Limited power ....

7. Crystal clear ....

8. Easy sailing ....

9. One's weak suit ....

10. Restricted power ....

11. Mutual praise ....

12. The thing you love most ....

13. Decent in expression ....

14. Something in which one is unskilled ....

15. In a healthy state ....

16. Stubborn ....

17. Not the least bit hazy ....

18. Exoteric ....

19. Keeps you awake ....

20. Marriage of white to white ....

ANSWERS: 1-esoteric; 2-miscegenation; 3-incongruous; 4-soporific; 5-cadaverous; 6-carte blanche; 7-nebulous; 8-impasse; 9-forte; 10-carte blanche; 11-recriminations; 12-bête noire; 13-scurrilous; 14-forte; 15-moribund; 16-docile; 17-nebulous; 18-esoteric; 19-soporific; 20-miscegenation

---

VI. It is extraordinarily difficult to write the definition of a word. And yet your understanding of a word must be somewhat nebulous if you can't define it. Try your hand at writing brief definitions of the following words.

Word	Definition
1. bête noire	....
2. cadaverous	....
3. carte blanche	....
4. esoteric	....
5. forte	....
6. impasse	....
7. incongruous	....
8. docile	....
9. miscegenation	....
10. moribund	....
11. nebulous	....
12. recriminations	....

13. repercussions ....

14. scurrilous ....

15. soporific ....

ANSWERS:

1. A person or object of fear or aversion; a bugbear.
2. Pale, ghastly, corpse-like.
3. An order signed in blank; unconditional authority.
4. Adapted exclusively for the initiated and enlightened few.
5. Your strong point; that skill in which you excel.
6. An impassable road or way; a blind alley; an insurmountable situation.
7. Out of place; inharmonious.
8. Easily led and managed.
9. Marriage between people of two different races; mixed marriage.
10. In a dying state.
11. Hazy; cloudy; amorphous.
12. Accusations repelled by other accusations; abusive arguments.
13. Reverberations; echoes.
14. Coarse, opprobrious abuse.
15. Tending to cause or to produce sleep.

You have learned the words in this chapter in the way that you normally learn words in your everyday life. That is, you first come across a new word in a book or in your newspaper, or you hear someone speak it. You wonder at its meaning. Your understanding of the word gradually clears and each time you see or hear it again, you find that your knowledge of it is becoming more secure. Finally you learn to know it so well that you dare to use it in your writing and speaking. You might even be able to define it, as you have done in this chapter, if you were called upon to do so, although this is the hardest challenge of all. That is, the methods we are using in this book are the methods that nature uses in teaching you your native language.

WORDS THAT DESCRIBE YOU

Keep in mind this important point in reference to your vocabulary improvement program. If you can personalize your new words, if you can make them bear some relationship to yourself and your way of living, you then materially increase your chances of making these words a *permanent* part of your vocabulary.

You can not learn words in a vacuum. That is, if a word can not be made to have a bearing on your life, if it can not be brought within the circle of your own thoughts, if it can not be made a part of your own personality or of your attitudes, then that word will remain useless to you.

The words in this chapter should, therefore, be thought of in reference to *yourself*. Let us, for the next few pages, consider your own attitudes towards Life.

1. Do you view with a certain degree of tolerance the eccentricities and foibles of other humans? Are you broadminded, sympathetic, inclined to see the other person's point of view? Do your tastes cover a wide range? For example, in your reading, can you be interested in everything from detective stories to Russian novels? In your eating, do your likes run the gamut from a New England dinner of boiled beef to a gourmet's delight of exotic sea food?

Yes? Then we will characterize you as a person whose tastes, interests, desires, and sympathies, are, in one word *catholic* (cath'-o-lik).

2. Do you make trouble by your unreasoning, irascible and vainglorious patriotism? Do you carry your jealousy of your country's honor to an absurd and ridiculous extreme? You are *chauvinistic* (sho-vin-ist'-ik).

3. Are you inclined to give up the struggle before the battle is lost? Are you all too ready to lay down your arms and admit defeat at a time when braver and more optimistic souls would see many reasons for carrying on? You are a *defeatist* (de-feet'-ist).

4. Do you like to dabble in the arts or the sciences? Fool a little bit with photography, only to abandon it, say for stamp collecting? If you flit like a butterfly from interest to interest, never concentrating for any length of time on one, you are a *dilettante* (dil-et-tan'-tee).

5. Are you one whose main purpose in life seems to be the attainment of pleasure? Do you put too high a value on the luxuries of life? Are you fond of eating and drinking and are you an expert in the choice of wines and foods? You are an *epicurean* (ep-i-kyoo-ree'-an).

6. Perhaps you find yourself in such a position, financially, that you must calculate closely the money costs of all your activities. Then, of course, you must practice economy. But are you *too* close-fisted with money? Do people call you stingy? You are *parsimonious* (par-si-mo'-nee-us).

7. Do you look with contempt upon artists and those with an artistic temperament? Are you ignorant? Preju-

diced? Blindly conventional? Narrow-minded? Do you tend to have low aims in life and are you inclined to be materialistic? You are a *philistine* (fil-iss'-tin).

8. Are you wasteful, extravagant, inclined to spend your money, time, energy, and talent without care or thought? You are a *profligate* (prof'-li-gat).

9. Do you meet the tragedies of life with a stiff upper lip? Do you conceal your emotions, no matter how great your mental or physical suffering may be? You are a *stoic* (sto'-ik).

10. Finally, do you happen to know a man who is so absurdly and slavishly devoted to his wife that he is the joke of the neighborhood? He is *uxorious* (ux-o'-ree-us).

II. When you have familiarized yourself with the meanings of all of the above words, you will be ready to try your wits on the following exercises. Each word or phrase describes or defines one of ten words that have been discussed in this chapter. Can you write the proper word in the proper place?

A-1. A dabbler in art matters   ....

2. Undue sparingness in money   ....

3. Narrow-minded; uncultured   ....

4. Always expecting failure   ....

5. With liberal views and wide tastes   ....

B-1. Niggardly ....
  2. Exaggeratedly patriotic ....
  3. Foolishly devoted to one's wife ....
  4. Believes that pleasure is chief good ....
  5. Recklessly extravagant ....

C-1. Absurdly nationalistic ....
  2. Materialistic ....
  3. "Give up the ship!" ....
  4. Stingy ....
  5. Superficial amateur ....

D-1. Penny-pinching ....
  2. Indifference to pleasure or pain ....
  3. A severe ascetic ....
  4. Ignorant and narrow-minded ....
  5. Given to dissipation ....

E-1. Comprehensive in sympathies ....
  2. Follows a branch of knowledge superficially ....
  3. Loves the refinements of pleasure ....
  4. Excessively patriotic ....
  5. "Eat and be merry!" ....

F-1. With exquisite taste in food and drink ....
  2. Abandoned in character and principles ....

3. Insensible to virtue and decency   ....

4. Wasteful of money   ....

5. Excessively fond of one's wife   ....

ANSWERS: A-1-dilettante; 2-parsimonious; 3-philistine; 4-defeatist; 5-catholic

B-1-parsimonious; 2-chauvinistic; 3-uxorious; 4-epicurean; 5-profligate

C-1-chauvinistic; 2-philistine; 3-defeatist; 4-parsimonious; 5-dilettante

D-1-parsimonious; 2-stoic; 3-stoic; 4-philistine; 5-profligate

E-1-catholic; 2-dilettante; 3-epicurean; 4-chauvinistic; 5-epicurean

F-1-epicurean; 2-profligate; 3-profligate; 4-profligate; 5-uxorious

———————

III. Each of the nine paragraphs that follow describes some one of the words that we have been talking about. Can you tell which one and write it in?

1. My taste is highly cultivated for all things. While I am not by any means promiscuous in my interests, still I can always see the other person's point of view. I am tolerant to a great degree, for my sympathies are comprehensive and all embracing. I am ....

2. Frugal? To the last ditch! People have even accused me of being tight-fisted and stingy, and I am afraid that if they are referring to my attitude toward spending money, they are correct. I am ....

3. I have been accused of being without emotions, but the fact is that I have merely trained myself to be indifferent alike to pain and pleasure. I am a (an) ....

4. I am greatly interested in the fine arts, but being a person of independent means I don't have to really work hard at them, and it isn't necessary for me to make a living out of them. They are more or less of a pastime with me. I am a (an) ....

5. My country? The best, the finest, the truest, the richest, the bravest, and if you don't think so you had better keep away from me. Why, I can scarcely find adjectives to describe my pride in my birthplace or to show the utter contempt I feel for all other lands. I am ....

6. I don't think it's fair to call me a traitor to my ideals. It's just that I do not care to fight what I know to be a losing battle. I am a (an) ....

7. Other people can waste time pampering artists and poets if they want to, but give me a he-man every time—the kind who is interested in material things like making money. And while we're on the subject, those people who keep their noses buried in books all the time, and who are always worrying about knowledge and progress and liberalism! Well, I can put them also on my list of people who won't be missed! I am a (an) ....

8. Laugh at me if you like and say that my wife uses me as a footstool. I don't care! Nothing I do will ever be good enough for her! I am ....

9. As for me, I like my pleasure. Other people can work and slave and worry about the future and save their

money, but not I! Give me a good time any day! Let the little milquetoasts keep their noses to the grindstone and lead temperate lives. I figure money is made to spend and I believe in the old proverb, "Eat, drink, and be merry." I am a (an) ....

ANSWERS: 1-catholic; 2-parsimonious; 3-stoic; 4-dilettante; 5-chauvinistic; 6-defeatist; 7-philistine; 8-uxorious; 9-epicurean

---

IV. Check the correct answer—either a, b or c—in each of the following.

1. A person of *catholic* tastes is
    a. religious
    b. moral
    c. sympathetic

2. If you met an American *chauvinist* it would be safe to remark:
    a. "I would really rather live abroad."
    b. "I love my country and I despise all other nations."
    c. "Listen, America has plenty of black marks on her record! How about the Spanish-American war?"

3. The *defeatist* is a
    a. coward
    b. pessimist
    c. bully

4. Anybody knows that a *dilettante* is
    a. a master of the arts

b. a struggling young artist
c. one who follows the arts as a pastime

5. The *epicurean's* greatest delight comes from
   a. pleasure
   b. cruelty
   c. self-torment

6. *Parsimonious?* He's a
   a. miser
   b. spendthrift
   c. philanthropist

7. While the word *philistine* is of Biblical origin, it now merely refers to a person who is
   a. hypocritically pious
   b. narrow-minded; opposed to progress and learning
   c. wealthy and hard-hearted

8. Few people realize that a *stoic* doesn't mind
   a. pleasure and pain
   b. spending money
   c. getting drunk

9. An *uxorious* man
   a. foolishly and fondly dotes on his wife
   b. is completely penniless
   c. always complains of the way life treats him

10. A *profligate* person is
    a. dishonest
    b. insincere
    c. wasteful

ANSWERS: 1-c; 2-b; 3-b; 4-c; 5-a; 6-a; 7-b; 8-a; 9-a; 10-c

V. *Definitions:* Write the correct word next to its definition.

1. Broad-minded in views   ....

2. An exaggerated patriot   ....

3. Follows the policy or practice of admitting defeat too quickly   ....

4. One who dabbles in art and letters   ....

5. One who makes a profession of pleasure. A connoisseur of food and wine   ....

6. Unnecessarily saving   ....

7. A person with a plebeian type of mind. An individual of materialistic tastes who is interested neither in art nor letters   ....

8. Completely given up to dissipation; dissolute; wasteful   ....

9. A person showing no emotion over pleasure or pain   ....

10. Extravagantly submissive to one's wife ....

ANSWERS: 1-catholic; 2-chauvinist; 3-defeatist; 4-dilettante; 5-epicurean; 6-parsimonious; 7-philistine; 8-profligate; 9-stoic; 10-uxorious

———

In all likelihood this has not been an easy chapter. But it is true, isn't it, that all learning and all the skills are only acquired by dogged, systematic and intensive work? After all, the greatest obstacle to anyone's getting ahead is just plain laziness. The average man makes a fair success with very ordinary effort, and conversely, most people lose out in life just because they won't take the trouble to win. That's why there's always so much room at the top.

If you will make use of the ideas in this book they will open many doors to you. If you will make the precepts of this book a lifetime habit, the habit will take care of you, and lead you to greater success. Success itself is a habit.

Life has many prizes waiting for the winner. And, after all, it's a lot less exhausting to win than to worry.

FRENCH PHRASES YOU CAN USE

The rivers of all languages have flowed into the vast reservoir of English.

The following paragraph will give you just a hint of its varied sources. Each of the italicized words came into English from a foreign language.

"The *sky* was teeming rain. The *boss* had a touch of *influenza*. He came up on the *verandah*, put down his *mammoth umbrella*, entered the comfortable *oasis* of his living-room and sat down. He filled his pipe with *tobacco*, warmed himself first with hot *cocoa*, then *coffee*, and listened to his pet *canary* sing."

Here are the parentages of these words:

sky ....Old Norse	umbrella ....Italian
boss ....Dutch	oasis ....Egyptian
influenza ....Italian	tobacco ......West Indian
verandah ......Portuguese	cocoa ....Mexican
mammoth ....Russian	coffee ....Arabic
canary ....Spanish	

The main contributors to English, however, are not the languages from which the above examples have been taken. They are, rather, French and Latin.

French, as would be understandable, has added a large number of delicate and graceful words and phrases to our speech. Many of these have been adopted so recently that they still retain their Gallic flavor.

I. Here are ten common French importations:

1. If a prisoner of war were being tortured and were on the point of death, the final stroke that killed him would be the *coup de grâce* (koo de grahss'). Any blow that puts a suffering and greatly weakened animal, person or institution out of its misery is a *coup de grâce*. Thus, we will say, a conqueror has allowed a subject nation to continue, for a time, with nominal independence. When and if that conqueror decides to over-run the vanquished nation and completely destroy its last vestige of freedom he will be delivering the *coup de grâce*.

2. Anyone who is in the way, out of place or not wanted is *de trop* (de tro'). If little brother insists on sitting in the living room when his sister's beau comes a-calling he is considered *de trop*.

3. In a sophisticated conversation slightly off-color or improper remarks are sometimes made in terms that seem innocent. Any word or phrase which has two meanings, one of them an indelicate one, is called a *double entendre* (doo'-ble ahn-tahn'-dre).

4. You are *en rapport* (ahn ra-por') with someone when there is a perfect meeting of minds and a complete absence of friction.

5. A real cooperative spirit on the part of a group, combined with an enthusiastic submergence of self-interest for

the sake of the common good, is called *esprit de corps* (esspree' de cor'). A crack regiment is sometimes famed for its *esprit de corps*.

6. Napoleon proved himself to be a leader *par excellence* (par ek-sel-ahnss'). Escoffier, noted the world over for his cuisine, was a chef *par excellence*. Ralph Waldo Emerson, we might say, was the interpreter of Plato *par excellence*.

7. If your mind is perfectly attuned to your surroundings, if you are alive and alert to all that is going on around you, if you are on guard, wide awake, eager, expectant, you are on the *qui vive* (kee veev').

8. A medley of things, an assorted and heterogeneous mixture of great variety, is called a *pot pourri* (po pooree').

9. and 10. Have you ever met a man or woman with perfect poise? Do you notice how he or she says exactly the correct and charming thing at the proper time? Never is such a person guilty of a *faux pas* (foe pah'), an embarrassing mistake; on the contrary, your perfectly poised, sophisticated, cosmopolitan friend is the possessor of *savoir faire* (sav-wahr fair').

The literal translations of these ten French terms will help establish the meanings in your mind. A little rehearsal of the pronunciations of these colorful words wouldn't be out of order.

1. Coup de grâce (koo de
   grahss') ....Blow of mercy
2. De trop (de tro') ....Too much

3. Double entendre (doo'-ble
   ahn-tahn'-dre) ....Double meaning
4. En rapport (ahn ra-por') ....Harmony of relation
5. Esprit de corps (ess-pree'-
   de cor') ....Spirit of the body
6. Par excellence (par ek-sel-
   ahnss') ....By excellence
7. Qui vive (kee veev') ....Who lives
8. Pot pourri (po poo-ree') ....Rotten pot
9. Faux pas (foe pah') ....False step
10. Savoir faire (sav-wahr
    fair') ....To know how to do

II. The ten words of this chapter have not been defined
for you as yet. Their meanings have at most been sketched
in. Nevertheless a careful re-reading of Section I will no
doubt make it possible for you to write the correct French
terms next to each of the following synonyms or synonymous phrases. Some of the terms we have just had will be
called for many times in the lists that are given below.

Sec. A 1. Out of place ....

      2. Group enthusiasm ....

      3. Double meaning ....

      4. Surpassingly good ....

      5. On the alert ....

ANSWERS: 1-de trop; 2-esprit de corps; 3-double entendre; 4-par
        excellence; 5-on the qui vive

How did the answers check with what you had written? Then let's see how many of the following sections you can fill in from memory.

Sec. B.   1. In the very choicest manner ....

        2. In agreement ....

        3. In the way ....

        4. Mixture ....

        5. Decisive blow ....

Sec. C   1. On your toes ....

        2. Two's company ....

        3. Finishing stroke ....

        4. Pre-eminently ....

        5. Off-color ambiguity ....

Sec. D   1. In harmonious relationship ....

        2. On guard ....

        3. Jealous regard for the honor of the group ....

        4. Medley ....

        5. Embarrassing error ....

Sec. E   1. Poise ....

        2. Little of everything ....

        3. In accord ....

4. Knowing and doing the graceful
thing   ....

5. Embarrassing mistake   ....

ANSWERS: *B*-1-par excellence; 2-en rapport; 3-de trop; 4-pot
pourri; 5-coup de grâce

C-1-on the qui vive; 2-de trop; 3-coup de grâce; 4-par
excellence; 5-double entendre

D-1-en rapport; 2-on the qui vive; 3-esprit de corps;
4-pot pourri; 5-faux pas

E-1-savoir faire; 2-pot pourri; 3-en rapport; 4-savoir
faire; 5-faux pas

———————

III. *True or False?* Below you will find ten statements,
in which the French words and phrases we have been
studying are used, some true, others false. Write T or F
next to each statement indicating whether you believe the
French words have been used correctly or not.

1. The fall of France was in the nature of a *coup
de grâce* for England.   ....

2. We found the Chinese *de trop* in our war
against Japan.   ....

3. Naïve girls indulge in frequent *doubles en-
tendres*.   ....

4. A husband and wife should be *en rapport*. ....

5. A defeated army is full of *esprit de corps*. ....

6. Sarah Bernhardt was admitted to be an actress
par excellence.   ....

7. A book of famous quotations is a *pot pourri* of literary gems. ....

8. A prize-fighter must be on the *qui vive* when he is in the ring. ....

9. A finishing school claims to give young girls *savoir faire*. ....

10. A *faux pas* is generally embarrassing. ....

ANSWERS: 1-F; 2-F; 3-F; 4-T; 5-F; 6-T; 7-T; 8-T; 9-T; 10-T

———

IV. Now we will give you the definitions. Can you match the French terms with them and write them down in their correct places below?

1. The mortal stroke. ....

2. Said of a person who is in the way, out of place or not wanted. ....

3. A word or phrase with double meaning. ....

4. In harmonious relation one with the other. ....

5. The common devotion of members to an organization. ....

6. Pre-eminent; beyond comparison. ....

7. A mixture; a medley; a melange. ....

8. The challenge of a French sentinel, meaning "Who goes there?" Hence, on the alert. ....

9. The ability to say and do the right thing at the right time. ....

10. A misstep; an embarrassing mistake. ....

ANSWERS: 1-coup de grâce; 2-de trop; 3-double entendre; 4-en
rapport; 5-esprit de corps; 6-par excellence; 7-pot
pourri; 8-qui vive; 9-savoir faire; 10-faux pas

These ten phrases are only a few of the thousands of
French words that have become the adopted children of
our language. Used with discretion, they can take their
places as the grace notes of cultured conversation and
writing. If you haven't already been introduced to them
you will be surprised how many you will hear or find if
you start listening or watching for them.

WORDS ABOUT WORDS

Every specialty, naturally, has its own terminology. The lawyers, the preachers, the doctors, all speak their own language. The physician, for instance, has to know the names of 707 different arteries, 71 bones, 79 convolutions, 433 muscles, 230 nerves, 403 veins, 295 poisons, 109 tumors and also about 10,000 drugs.

The philologist speaks his own language, too, and unless we were versed in his speech we would find it difficult to understand him when he talked of phonology, phonemics and morphology.

We can, however, pick a few of the more popular words that lie in this field of language, ones that we can use in common conversation. For some of the most interesting words in our language are words about words. Here, below, are ten such.

I. 1. anticlimax (an-ti-klye′-max)
    2. analogy (a-nal′-o-jee)
    3. ambiguity (am-bi-gyoo′-i-tee)
    4. cliché (klee-shay′)
    5. epigram (ep′-i-gram)
    6. euphemism (you′-fe-mizm)
    7. redundancy (ree-dun′-dan-see)
    8. non sequitur (non sek′-wi-toor)

9. persiflage (per-si-flazh')
10. simile (sim'-i-lee)

And now here is an example of each:

II. 1. *Anticlimax*
Dr. Jones and Dr. Smith will be guest speakers at the County Medical Society meeting Tuesday night at Mineola. Dr. Jones will take his topic from the Psalms: "Behold how good and pleasant it is for brethren to dwell together in unity." Dr. Smith will speak on "flat feet."

2. *Analogy*
Your body is like a machine. Put in the proper fuel and it will function efficiently.

3. *Ambiguity*
The farmer's helper took his car out of the garage. (Whose car did he take?)

4. *Cliché*
"It's a great life if you don't weaken."

5. *Epigram*
It is more blessed to give than to receive.

6. *Euphemism*
"Mortician" or "funeral director" for undertaker or embalmer.

7. *Redundancy*
   The biggest, the greatest, the most stupendous show
   on earth.

8. *Non Sequitur*
   "Despite her age, her interest in music never flagged.
   During the past year she has crocheted a bedspread
   and a table-cloth."

9. *Persiflage*
   "Man never knows precisely what is right
   So, torn between a purpose and a doubt,
   He first makes windows to let in the light,
   And then hangs curtains up to shut it out."

10. *Simile*
    As thick as sea-gulls on a rock.

III. If some of these words are not a part of your normal
     and familiar vocabulary, the following problems may
     be hard for you to solve. Try, anyhow, to fill in the
     blank spaces. There will be a very real virtue in mak-
     ing the attempt, and with each attempt the meaning
     of the unknown word will become more clear.

1. Change *anticlimax* to an adjective, filling the form into
   the following sentence:
   After the great naval victory, the sinking of a single
   enemy trawler was ....

2. Change *analogy* to an adjective:
   Let us discuss an .... situation.
3. Change *ambiguity* to an adjective:
   That is an .... statement.
4. *Cliché* has no other common forms.
5. Change *epigram* to an adjective:
   Oscar Wilde has an .... style.
6. Change *euphemism* to an adjective:
   Let us use a more .... term.
7. Change *redundancy* to an adjective:
   Your statement is ....
8. *Non sequitur* has no other common forms.
9. *Persiflage* has no other common forms.
10. *Simile* has no other common forms.

ANSWERS: 1-anticlimactic; 2-analogous (an-al′-o-gus); 3-ambigu-
         ous (am-big′-you-us); 4-none; 5-epigrammatic; 6-
         euphemistic; 7-redundant; 8-none; 9-none; 10-none

———————

IV. Now we will give you, for the first time, the dictionary
    definitions. The meanings of any words that are
    strange may be hard to identify. The problem is to
    write in each word after the definition that you believe
    describes it. As a valid test to your understanding, try
    to fill them in without referring to the previous pages.

    1. A rhetorical figure expressing comparison
       or likeness   ....
    2. Partial agreement or resemblance between
       things somewhat different; similarity in
       certain aspects   ....

3. A light, flippant style of conversation or writing; banter; raillery ....

4. A stale, worn-out or stereotyped phrase, either written or spoken ....

5. An inference, or conclusion, that does not follow from the facts as stated ....

6. A gradual or sudden decrease in the importance or impressiveness of what is said; the opposite of climax; a ludicrous or ridiculous drop in thought and expression, sometimes from the sublime to the ridiculous ....

7. Vagueness; indefiniteness; uncertainty; an expression whose meaning can be taken in two or more ways ....

8. A pithy saying in prose or verse that crystallizes a wise or witty thought ....

9. A pleasing expression used in place of one which is plainer or more accurate but which might be offensive, embarrassing, or in bad taste ....

10. Most commonly used to mean unnecessary repetition or the employment of more words than are necessary ....

ANSWERS: 1-simile; 2-analogy; 3-persiflage; 4-cliché; 5-non sequitur; 6-anticlimax; 7-ambiguity; 8-epigram; 9-euphemism; 10-redundancy

———————

V. The following is an assignment that you can do or not as your time and enthusiasm permit. It will be of great advantage to you, though, if you can put newly learned words to immediate use.

Would you like to write a sample phrase illustrating each of the words you have just had? Your results, of course, do not have to be scintillating or original. Compare your answers with the examples in Section II.

1. Anticlimax

2. Analogy

3. Ambiguity

4. Cliché

5. Epigram

6. Euphemism

7. Redundancy

8. Non sequitur

9. Persiflage

10. Simile

VI. If we are to trace the ancestry of such words as those given above we can often throw a new light on their meanings, or at least we can dramatize them and make them vivid. Here are the sources, all but one of them Latin and Greek, of the ten "words about words."

1. *Anticlimax:* From the Greek *anti,* "opposite to" and *klimax,* "ladder." So an "anticlimax" is really the opposite of climbing up; that is, it is climbing *down* the ladder!

2. *Analogy:* The Greek *ana,* "according to" plus *logos,* "proportion." Things "analogous" to each other, while different, are similar in proportion.

3. *Ambiguity:* Latin *ambi,* "around," plus *agere,* "to go." When you make an "ambiguous" statement you are going around the subject!

4. *Cliché:* A French word that means "an electrotype or stereotype plate for printing." This is why a statement of yours that is stereotyped, fixed and lacking in originality is called a "cliché."

5. *Epigram:* The Greek *epi,* "on" and *graphe,* "write."

6. *Euphemism:* Greek *eu,* "well"; *phemi,* "speak." So if you utter a "euphemism" you are at least making an effort to give a nice turn to a subject that would otherwise be disagreeable.

7. *Redundancy:* From the Latin *re,* "back" and *unda,* "wave." The waves are driven back on the shore and repeat themselves like your words when you are "redundant."

8. *Non sequitur:* The direct translation from the Latin literally means "it does not follow."

9. *Persiflage:* From the Latin *per,* meaning "through" and *sibilare,* "to hiss" or "whistle." Possibly, since "persiflage" sometimes means banter there may be a significance in the fact that whistling or hissing can be sounds of derision.

10. *Simile:* From the Latin *similis,* meaning "similar."

The entire list of "words about words" would, of course, fill a small dictionary. The Greeks, for instance, laid the foundation of our grammar, and, therefore, in discussions of literary style the Greek roots predominate, such as *trope, rhetoric, onomatopoeia, synecdoche, trochee, syntax.*

In the confines of this book we can only *introduce* the reader to the vocabularies that group themselves around the various departments of his life. We hope that the student will be encouraged to search out other words in these fields.

WORD BUILDING BY THE
"UNFOLDING PROCESS"

Let us now approach the problem of word development from a slightly different direction. We will still rely on the indirect method: that is, the method that shows you a word first in its context, rather than flashing it on you alone and away from its meaning in a sentence.

The meanings and uses of the following group of difficult words will be revealed by what we might call, for want of a better name, the "unfolding process." As you meet each word, even though it is for the first time, its meaning will be partially shown to you by the context, and its full meaning will gradually unfold before the chapter is over.

I. Please read out loud each of the sentences given below, so that you may get at least a feeling for the italicized words. You may still be completely in the dark as to the meaning of a few of them.

1. He lives a severe and *abstemious* (ab-stee'-mee-us) life.

2. That is a *chimerical* (ki-mair'-ik-al) and wholly unfounded fear.

3. The mental alertness you acquire is an important *facet* (fass'-et) of improved vocabulary.

4. Honesty is a *fetish* (fee'-tish) with him.

5. The *Machiavellian* (mack-ee-a-vell'-ee-an) moves of the dictators are astounding.

6. *Ochlocracy* (ok-lock'-ra-see) is usually one result of war.

7. Only God in his wisdom is *omniscient* (om-nish'-ent).

8. Since John's treachery was discovered, he has become a *pariah* (pa'-ree-a).

9. The employee received a *peremptory* (per'-emp-toe-ree) dismissal.

10. The refugee painted a *poignant* (poyn'-ant) picture of his sufferings.

11. The wife of Socrates was sour and *querulous* (kwer'-ul-us).

12. That is the most ridiculous and *specious* (spee'-shus) argument I have ever listened to.

13. The war fever in 1941 was *ubiquitous* (you-bick'-wi-tus).

14. He is so *unctuous* (unk'-choo-us), I cannot bear him.

15. That *vainglorious* (vain-glo'-ree-us) and pompous general annoys all who know him.

II. Some of these words may already be old friends of yours, and an actual part of your speaking vocabulary. With others you may be only partially acquainted, and some could easily be entirely unfamiliar to you. The following exercise will be another step towards a clarification of the unfamiliar ones.

Let's start with the first. Directly after "1. abstemious" you will find three words identified with the letters "a, b and c." One of these words is a synonym for "abstemious." Check whichever one you think it is. Please continue the process with the fifteen words. Refer back to Section I when you wish to.

1. *abstemious*
   a. licentious   b. miserly   c. sparing

2. *chimerical*
   a. monstrous   b. fanciful   c. difficult

3. *facet*
   a. side   b. tap   c. point of view

4. *fetish*
   a. shoe   b. object of worship   c. love

5. *Machiavellian*
   a. kingly   b. politically cunning   c. angelic

6. *ochlocracy*
   a. dictatorship   b. mob-rule   c. democracy

7. *omniscient*
   a. omnipotent   b. rare   c. all-knowing

8. *pariah*
   a. outcast   b. invisible   c. traitor

9. *peremptory*
   a. tardy   b. fearful   c. decisive

10. *poignant*
    a. piquant   b. painfully mov-   c. bitter
                        ing

11. *querulous*
    a. questioning   b. complaining   c. fretful

12. *specious*
    a. remarkable   b. cunning   c. subtly false

13. *ubiquitous*
    a. ecstatic   b. omnipresent   c. pestiferous

14. *unctuous*
    a. dirty   b. unconcerned   c. making a bland
                                            pretense of spir-
                                            ituality

15. *vainglorious*
    a. silly   b. boastful   c. fastidious

ANSWERS: 1-(c); 2-(b); 3-(a); 4-(b); 5-(b); 6-(b); 7-(c); 8-(a);
         9-(c); 10-(b); 11-(b); 12-(c); 13-(b); 14-(c); 15-(b)

───────────────

Please recheck your answers and correct your mistakes
if you have made any. Also go back to Section I on each
of your mistakes and note the new meanings the sentences
have once the word is properly understood.

III. Now we are going to ask you to think *in reverse*.
The more angles from which we approach these words,
the more the words will become fixed in your mind.

It is only fair to warn you that this will be an extremely
difficult exercise, and one in which the most alert mind
can easily be tricked.

Below you will find in italics the fifteen words you have just covered. After each master word there are three other words lettered "a, b and c."

Let's start with the first one, "1. abstemious." Three words follow this: "a. miserly, b. prodigal, c. philanthropic." One of these three words is directly *opposite* in meaning to abstemious. Check the one that you think is the antonym, or opposite in meaning, and repeat this process with the whole list of fifteen words. We have put in some synonyms to fool you, but don't be trapped by them!

1. *abstemious*
   a. miserly   b. prodigal   c. philanthropic
2. *chimerical*
   a. harmless   b. real   c. ghastly
3. *facet*
   This word has no antonym
4. *fetish*
   a. amulet   b. object of hate   c. rosary
5. *Machiavellian*
   a. noxious   b. happy   c. naïve
6. *ochlocracy*
   a. rule by one b. rule by the rich   c. rule by the intelligent
7. *omniscient*
   a. all-seeing   b. ignorant   c. religious
8. *pariah*
   a. leper   b. hero   c. idol
9. *peremptory*
   a. debatable   b. temporary   c. slow
10. *poignant*
    a. sharp   b. dull   c. immature

11. *querulous*
    a. calm   b. satisfied   c. peaceful
12. *specious*
    a. general   b. authentic   c. hesitant
13. *ubiquitous*
    a. found no-   b. found every-   c. humorous
       where   where
14. *unctuous*
    a. crude   b. suave   c. ignorant
15. *vainglorious*
    a. modest   b. boastful   c. plaintive

ANSWERS: 1-(b); 2-(b); 3-This word has no antonym; 4-(b);
      5-(c); 6-(a); 7-(b); 8-(c); 9-(a); 10-(b); 11-(b);
      12-(b); 13-(a); 14-(a); 15-(a)

———————

IV. The unfamiliar words may now be getting more
under your control. In the exercise that follows try to
write the proper word (saying it aloud as you do so) in
the space allowed for it next to each of the synonyms or
synonymous phrases.

1. dictatorial ....   6. object of wor-
2. mob-rule ....   ship ....
3. outcast ....   7. painfully touch-
4. shrewdly cun-   ing ....
   ning ....   8. everywhere ....
5. all-knowing ....   9. one face of a
                                    gem ....

10. complaining ....

11. temperate   ....

12. true only in
    appearance ....

13. boastful   ....

14. foolishly fanci-
    ful   ....

15. showing a pre-
    tense of spirit-
    uality   ....

ANSWERS: 1-peremptory; 2-ochlocracy; 3-pariah; 4-Machiavel-
lian; 5-omniscient; 6-fetish; 7-poignant; 8-ubiquitous;
9-facet; 10-querulous; 11-abstemious; 12-specious;
13-vainglorious; 14-chimerical; 15-unctuous

V. Which word of those you have had does each of the
following phrases remind you of? Write the correct word
in its proper place.

1. Reign of terror during French Revolution   ....

2. An object of worship among savages   ....

3. An absurd creation of the imagination   ....

4. A leper   ....

5. A dictator's methods   ....

6. The arguments of a demagogue   ....

7. No spot in the empire was far removed
   from him. He seemed to be   ....

8. The suffering of a refugee   ....

9. Boastfulness was a characteristic of
   Napoleon   ....

10. A complaining wife   ....

11. Women who are on a reducing diet   ....

12. A diamond   ....

13. God   ....

14. A martinet's order to an underling   ....

15. A smooth appearance of sanctity   ....

ANSWERS: 1-ochlocracy; 2-fetish; 3-chimerical; 4-pariah; 5-
        Machiavellian; 6-specious; 7-ubiquitous; 8-poignant;
        9-vainglorious; 10-querulous; 11-abstemious; 12-facet;
        13-omniscient; 14-peremptory; 15-unctuous

VI. "Toujours la pratique" say the French—"Always the
practice." Let's turn these words a new way, for, unless
you are absolutely sure of them you will never use them
publicly. We have split the words up into four groups of
five each so that you can check your results as you go along.
Several of them are repeated. It will be your responsibility
to write in, in each blank space, the one word among
those you have been studying which will most aptly fit
the meaning.

Group 1

1. The refugees painted a .... picture of their suffering in Germany.

2. You may insist that everybody hates you and avoids you,
   but I assure you that's a .... of your diseased
   imagination.

3. That teacher makes a .... of discipline.

4. He is a glib, ... person; I do not trust him.

5. Your .... schemes to win the nomination will get you nowhere; already your name is anathema to most of your constituents.

ANSWERS: 1-poignant; 2-chimera; 3-fetish; 4-unctuous; 5-Machiavellian

---

Group 2

1. At Christmas time, the .... Salvation Army lassie reminds a selfish public of people for whom the season may not be merry.

2. That is a .... argument; but possibly you may get a number of unthinking people to believe it.

3. I admit you have done a lot for your country, but this absurd quality of .... with which you are obsessed will not make you popular.

4. Invalids, crotchety old men and women, seem peculiarly addicted to the quality of ....

5. There are so many .... to the international situation, that it is difficult to guess what the future holds.

ANSWERS: 1-ubiquitous; 2-specious; 3-vainglory; 4-querulousness; 5-facets

---

Group 3

1. No one knows what is going to happen in the world. Things are in such an imbroglio. One would have to be .... to know.

2. Poor people, through lack of money, are forced to be ....

3. Lynching is an excellent example of ....
4. Sometimes it is necessary for an author to know what is going on in the minds of his characters. This is called ....
5. After murdering Lincoln, John Wilkes Booth became a ....

ANSWERS: 1-omniscient; 2-abstemious; 3-ochlocracy; 4-omniscience; 5-pariah

---

Group 4

1. Some mothers make their commands so ...., that they antagonize their children.
2. He is winning you over to his side with .... reasoning.
3. His .... machinations make him the most feared and the least trusted man in America.
4. In the spring the color green may be said to be almost ....
5. Some housewives make an absolute .... out of neatness.

ANSWERS: 1-peremptory; 2-specious; 3-Machiavellian; 4-ubiquitous; 5-fetish

---

VII. The defining of any word is incredibly hard. Just think, for instance, of writing a definition of "sky" in such a way that a blind man will get a clear idea of what you mean. But your very attempt to define the fifteen words that are listed below will force you to think intensively about them and will hammer and clinch their meanings in your mind in a way that nothing else could possibly do. When you have finished please check your answers with the dictionary definitions on page 220. Your wording, of course, will be different, but if your definitions contain the main elements, you may certainly consider that you have substantially mastered the fifteen words.

Word	*Definition*
1. abstemious	....
2. chimerical	....
3. facet	....
4. fetish	....
5. Machiavellian	....
6. ochlocracy	....
7. omniscient	....
8. pariah	....
9. peremptory	....
10. poignant	....
11. querulous	....
12. specious	....
13. ubiquitous	....
14. unctuous	....
15. vainglorious	....

ANSWERS:

1. Eating and drinking sparingly; self-denying in the indulgence of the appetites and passions.

2. Merely imaginary; fanciful; fantastic; visionary. The noun means a frightful, vain, or foolish fancy.

3. One of the small surfaces cut upon a diamond or other gem. By extension, a part, aspect, or point of view of any large subject.

4. A material object believed to be the dwelling of a spirit that will protect the owner from harm; any object of devotion or blind affection.

5. Of or pertaining to the Florentine politician Niccolo Machiavelli, or to a system of political trickery.

6. Mob-rule.

7. All-knowing, or all-wise.

8. A social outcast.

9. Positive in judgment or opinion; dogmatic; dictatorial.

10. Severely painful or acute to the spirit.

11. Disposed to complain or be fretful.

12. Appearing right and true; plausible.

13. Seeming to be everywhere at once; omnipresent.

14. Characterized by affected emotion; hence unduly suave.

15. Excessively proud of one's own attainments or accomplishments, or performance, as shown in undue elation, boasting.

This chapter has contained a few long and somewhat unusual words, and this leads us to a warning that we can't repeat too often. When we speak of the value of a large vocabulary we don't mean a vocabulary of *large* words. A large word has its place. Sometimes it will crystallize a meaning that otherwise might require a whole phrase to express. Fine. Use such a word then. It will make for brevity and clarity. It is much simpler to describe a man as a "monogamist" than to have to say that "he is the type of man who believes in marrying only one wife." But never use a long word when a short one will do. Never try for fancy phrases. Persons who do that are not being "literary." They are merely being stuffy and are attempting to parade their knowledge. Don't say, "I reside in my domicile." Say, "I *live* in my *house*." You don't commence; you *begin*. You don't pass away, or go to your reward; you *die*. A conflagration is a *fire*. And you don't retire; you just plain *go to bed*.

The highest art is usually the simplest in form, be it sculpture or music or architecture or painting or writing.

WORDS FROM CLASSIC ROOTS

We Americans are the most inventive nation in the world, and we have been applying this genius continually to our language. We have been inventing words ever since the Pilgrims drew lots for land, and began identifying a piece of ground as a "lot."

We have not only invented words, but, as has been indicated in this book, we have hungrily adopted them from other languages and have adapted the imported and foreign words to our own uses.

In this chapter we will explore several roads that branch off from the simple numbers *one, two* and *three*. You may find that we will repeat some etymological roots that we have already had.

I. The Greek word *monos,* "one," appears in English words as *mono* or *mon.* Thus a *monocle* is a glass for *one* eye. *Monogamy* is *one* marriage. A *monogram* is a combination of two or more letters so arranged as to represent a single unit.

Try to write in each of the eleven spaces below a word containing *mon* or *mono* that will fulfill in its meaning the definition or description that follows.

1. ....   A treatise on *one* subject

2. ....   A speech uttered by *one* person

3. ....   Mental derangement confined to *one* idea

4. ....   An airplane with *one* pair of wings

5. ....   Exclusive possession or control of any *one* thing

6. ....   A word of *one* syllable

7. ....   Belief in *one* god

8. ....   Uttered in *one* unvarying tone

9. ....   Government in the hands of *one* ruler

10. ....   A dwelling-place where each person under religious vows lives as *one*

11. ....   The inhabitant of such a house described in item 10

ANSWERS: 1-monograph; 2-monologue; 3-monomania; 4-mono-
plane; 5-monopoly; 6-monosyllable; 7-monotheism;
8-monotone, monotonous; 9-monarchy; 10-monastery;
11-monk

If we analyze some of the words in the previous exercise, we will discover that a number of new stems have
appeared.

1. In *monograph,* we have *graph,* a stem meaning "to
   write."
   Other examples:
   graphic—written; hence, vivid.

> *graphite*—writing material.
> *autograph*—written by oneself.
> *chirography*—handwriting.
> *telegraph*—writing far away.

2. From *monologue,* we can isolate the stem *logue* or *logy,* which is a Greek root which means "knowledge" or "discourse." We have learned, in Chapter 13, a body of words containing this root: entomo*logy,* philo*logy,* embryo*logy,* etymo*logy.* Others are:

> *dialogue*—discourse by two people.
> *eulogy*—good discourse.
> *biology*—knowledge or science of life.
> *trilogy*—discourse in three parts.

3. *Monomania* reminds us of other words containing the same root, *mania* "derangement":

> *dipsomania—kleptomania—pyromania—*
> *nymphomania—megalomania.*

4. *Monotheism* gives rise to other words containing the Greek root *theos,* "god":

> *polytheism—theology—theocracy—atheism.*

II. *Bi* is a prefix from the Latin, and denotes "two." Thus, *biannual,* "twice" a year; *bicameral,* with "two" houses, as the Senate and the House of Representatives in our Congress, or the House of Lords and the House of Commons in England; *biceps,* a muscle having "two" heads of origin; *bicuspid,* a tooth ending in "two" points.

Can you write in the following spaces ten other forms with *bi*?

1. .... A vehicle with *two* wheels

2. .... Occurring every *two* years

3. .... Eyeglasses having *two* kinds of lenses

4. .... *Second* marriage while the first is still in effect

5. .... Every *two* months

6. .... Something used for *two* eyes

7. .... An animal with *two* feet

8. .... Something cooked *twice,* i.e., a cracker

9. .... Cut into *two* parts

10. .... A marine animal with *two* shells, as an oyster, clam, etc.

ANSWERS: 1-bicycle; 2-biennial; 3-bifocals; 4-bigamy; 5-bi-monthly; 6-binoculars; 7-biped; 8-biscuit; 9-bisect; 10-bivalve

———————

A brief examination of the above words will introduce us to still other stems. For instance, we have:

1. *bicycle*—(*cycle,* "wheel")—tricycle, cycle
2. *bigamy*—(*gamy,* "marriage")—monogamy, polygamy
3. *binoculars*—(*ocul,* "eye")—oculist, monocle
4. *biped*—(*ped,* "foot")—pedal, quadruped
5. *bisect*—(*sect,* "cut")—insect, section

III. *Tri* is a Latin prefix meaning "three." Thus, in music, a *triad* is a chord of "three" notes; a *triangle* is a figure of "three" angles; a *tricolor* is a flag of "three" colors. Now fill in the twelve spaces with the proper words made up of *tri*.

1. .... A vehicle of *three* wheels
2. .... Having *three* sides
3. .... Made up of, or pertaining to, *three* languages
4. .... A series of *three* literary or musical compositions
5. .... Every *three* months
6. .... The union of *three* persons, as the Father, the Son, and the Holy Ghost
7. .... *Three* people who sing a song
8. .... Consisting of *three*
9. .... *Three* children born simultaneously from the same mother
10. .... A *three*-legged stand, as for a camera

ANSWERS: 1-tricycle; 2-trilateral; 3-trilingual; 4-trilogy; 5-trimonthly; 6-trinity; 7-trio; 8-triple; 9-triplets; 10-tripod

———

In the above words we can separate two more useful stems:

1. *later,* "side"; as in bi*later*al, a "two-sided" object—quadri*later*al, a "four-sided" object.

2. *pod,* "foot"; as in *pod*ium, the small raised platform on which the conductor of an orchestra stands—chiro*pod*ist and *pod*iatrist, the professional names of the doctors who take care of your feet. Incidentally *pod* is the Greek form of the stem which appeared in the Latin form *ped* in Section II of this chapter.

The following roots have been brought to our attention in this chapter. In order to further fix them in your mind will you try to fill in the two spaces that are allowed in each one of the following thirteen sections with two words based on the indicated root.

1. *mono,* one

   a. ....

   b. ....

2. *graph,* write

   a. ....

   b. ....

3. *logue,* discourse

   a. ....

   b. ....

4. *mania,* derangement

   a. ....

   b. ....

5. *theos,* god

   a. ....

   b. ....

6. *bi,* two

   a. ....

   b. ....

7. *cycle,* wheel

   a. ....

   b. ....

8. *gamy,* marriage

   a. ....

   b. ....

9. *ocul*, eye

   a. ....

   b. ....

10. *ped* or *pod*, foot

   a. ....

   b. ....

11. *sect*, cut

   a. ....

   b. ....

12. *tri*, three

   a. ....

   b. ....

13. *later*, side

   a. ....

   b. ....

If you are uncertain as to any of your answers please refer to the various sections of this chapter to check your results.

It is hardly necessary to point out how swiftly a student's vocabulary will expand if he will train himself to watch for Greek and Latin roots, to follow them up and to learn their meanings.

WORDS CHANGE THEIR MEANINGS

You may remember the anecdote that was told of King George the First of England and Sir Christopher Wren, the architect of St. Paul's Cathedral in London. Upon the completion of the masterly edifice the King told Wren that his work was "amusing, awful and artificial." Sir Christopher was delighted with the royal compliment, inasmuch as 300 years ago *amusing* meant *amazing, awful* meant *awe-inspiring,* and *artificial* meant *artistic.*

That is a dramatic indication of how the meanings of words change over the years. Latin and Greek, of course, are dead languages and are therefore static, but a language as vital and alive as English is in a constant state of flux.

In very olden days roses used to stink. This was not the fault of the flowers but of the word. In Old English "stink," and "stench" too, referred to any odor at all, good or bad. But since unpleasant odors make a stronger impression on us than others, and are, therefore, more often commented upon, the meaning of the word gradually shifted, and came finally to have only an unpleasant significance.

Similar shifts in meaning are occurring right under our eyes today. The words "smell" and "odor," when they are unqualified by adjectives, are beginning to gather about them disagreeable connotations. The phrases "what a smell" or "what an odor" certainly no longer refer to anything pleasant. Nowadays when our noses are pleased we have to resort to such terms as "scent" and "aroma." If these words become soiled, some day, as they almost surely will, we may find ourselves resorting to "bouquet," a word now largely restricted to the distinctive aroma of wine.

Oddly enough, the unattractive word "stink" has not yet stopped changing. Ever since the motion picture actor, Mischa Auer, delivered on thousands of silver screens throughout the nation, that famous remark "Confidentially, it stinks!" the word has taken a flagrant place in our language and has enjoyed a remarkable popularity with all classes—and with what meaning? It has become the most odorless of abstractions and is applied to anything that is extraordinarily bad in any way whatsoever. This word is now on the way to inclusion in the dictionary in its new sense.

"Villain" is another once respectable word that degenerated. Originally "a villain" was a farm laborer, or one who worked in a villa. Some philologists think it was helped in its downward path by its supposed connection with the unrelated word "vile." Likewise, "hussy," which means a fresh, pert, impudent girl, is merely a contraction of the innocent word "housewife."

"Starve" used to mean "die." "Zest" was a piece of lemon peel. "Meat" in Anglo-Saxon was any food at all, as in the Biblical "If meat maketh my brother to offend. . . ." In the sixteenth century "specious" meant "beautiful," "stupid" meant "amazed," and "mortified" meant "deadened." And when the American settlers founded Plymouth, "naughty" still meant just what it sounds like

—good for naught—and in the records of the colony we find the odd phrase, "small and naughty canoes."

Change is of course one of the most reliable indications of a healthy and growing language. And no language has ever grown so luxuriantly or changed so radically as English, or, its close cousin, our American language. It is changing day by day.

A few short years ago "broadcast" meant merely "to sow seed." Now it refers to the radio. "Exotic" meant "foreign or strange," as "an exotic flower." Now we speak of a motion picture actress as being "exotic" when she is glamorous, and the use even of "glamor" in this sense is as new as motion pictures.

In days such as these when history is being made so rapidly, our language changes at a quickened pace. There are two words, for instance, that at the moment are running a curious course. "Liquidate" is one. As we know, this word means "to settle a debt"; and yet we read that the dictator "liquidated" his generals. By no stretch of the imagination did "liquidate" ever mean "murder or kill" before, yet "murder or kill" it means now. "Purge" is another such word. When we read that the President attempted to "purge" a recalcitrant senator we are seeing the word used in a sense that it was never used in before. Nevertheless this new meaning of the word is already so clear to the average reader that the connection between "purge" and "purgative" meaning laxative probably never enters his mind.

English, like time, marches on. What a word meant yesterday it no longer means today. The word "humor" formerly referred to one's disposition or state of mind; earlier, it referred to one of the four fluids of the body, and *still* earlier, to moisture or vapor. Now it identifies that sense by aid of which we can appreciate something funny; and "funny," which once meant "laughable," now often means "queer or odd."

In the old days when we said a person was lying "prone" we meant, quite correctly, that he was lying on his face. Today, judging by newspaper photographs, he is usually lying on his back. In our present times a "fight" is often simply an argument; a "celebrity" is anyone who was in yesterday's gossip column. Today one can "climb up" as well as down; a "cavalcade" need not have a single horse in it; "lay" means "lie"; "fix" certainly means "repair"; and "quite," formerly meaning "wholly," now, like "awfully," often means only "very." "Acclimate" has changed its pronunciation as well as its meaning, and is now usually used to show adjustment not only to weather or physical conditions, but even to one's friends. "Asylum," which comes from the Greek *asylon,* "no right of seizure," meant originally "a place of refuge." In modern times this word has been so corrupted that it has signified only "lunatic asylum." Today when we are giving "asylum" to so many refugees, this word is beginning to revert to its original sense.

So our language shifts, changes, grows, and is alive to the finger-tips. There are new words for new times. If conditions today were identical with those of sixty years ago, a "cabriolet" would still mean a "light, one-horse, two-seated carriage" as it did to our great-grandfathers, and not a convertible automobile coupe. If civilization had not changed from Anglo-Saxon times, "curious" would still mean "careful," and "silly" would still mean "blessed."

You will find it a fascinating, and also invaluable game, if you will develop a practiced ability to watch for and to recognize these changes. While the object of this book has been to help you to enlarge your vocabulary, we, the authors, have also wished to make you more acutely word-conscious than you may ever have been before.

You have come now practically to the end of your course. The next chapter will be a review test. You will have some idea of the progress you have made when we tell you that, in these lessons, you have added more words to your vocabulary than the average adult adds during his entire life. After the middle twenties vocabulary growth virtually ceases unless a planned effort is made.

Remember how limited most of us are as to words. Nine native words, such as "it" and "the" make up one-quarter of our conversation. Add 34 more and you have half the words of our daily speech. That is, 43 words do fifty per cent of our conversational work. There is so little you have to do to beat this average.

Write it down in your primer that a mastery of words is one of the essentials in every sphere of life.

YOUR 30-DAY VOCABULARY TEST

You have now added the greater part of 500 usable and valuable words to your working vocabulary. It will be interesting to find out how many of them you are still sure of. It will not be surprising if you find yourself uncertain about a number of them. Let's check to see. Allow two points for each correct answer. You will find the answers on pages 247-249.

We have split this final test up into thirty parts for your convenience. The numbering of the sections bears no relation to the chapter numberings that have gone before. This examination does not cover all the words you have had, but it gives you a very thorough sampling.

Mark yourself, and see how you come out.

I. *Directions:* Check in each case a, b or c, the correct synonym for each italicized word.

1. *gregarious*
   a. home-loving   b. party-loving   c. food-loving

2. *wanton*
   a. unre-   b. desirous   c. useful
      strained

3. *pander*
   a. fry   b. cater to   c. raise

4. *effete*
   a. worn-out   b. strong   c. happy
      (as soil)

5. *vicarious*
   a. actual   b. second-hand   c. vicious

II. Write down five words ending in *mania*.

1.

2.

3.

4.

5.

III. Write five verbs for the following meanings. The initial letter is given in each case.

1. To spend time in the country   R ....

2. To delay   P ....

3. To show disapproval   D ....

4. To exclude from social privileges   O ....

5. To be bright and witty   S ....

IV. Write the title of the doctor you would see for each of these troubles.

1. Eye diseases   ....

2. Children's disease   ....

3. Organic mental disorder   ....

4. Skin trouble   ....

5. Crooked teeth   ....

V. Name the disease or the field each of these doctors specializes in.

1. Podiatrist   ....   4. Oculist   ....

2. Gynecologist   ....   5. Obstetrician   ....

3. Dermatologist   ....

VI. Check the correct synonyms, a, b or c, for each of the italicized words.

1. *panacea*
    a. theory   b. information   c. cure-all

2. *vindictive*
   a. revengeful   b. releasing   c. wise
3. *maudlin*
   a. tearfully   b. angry   c. happy
   sentimental
4. *misogynist*
   a. man-hater   b. marriage-hater   c. woman-hater
5. *vitriolic*
   a. glassy   b. caustic   c. mild

VII. Name the type of philosophy that is defined by each
     of the following words or phrases.

1. There is no God   ....

2. No one knows if God exists   ....

3. Belief that all virtue consists in self-interest ....

4. Indulgence in dainty appetites   ....

5. Excessive patriotism   ....

VIII. Name the field each of these scientists specializes in.

1. anthropologist .... 4. embryologist ....

2. geologist   .... 5. entomologist ....

3. archaeologist .... 6. ethnologist ....

7. etymologist .... 9. philologist ....

8. ornithologist .... 10. psychologist ....

IX. Write down in the blank spaces the verbs which best fit the definitions.

1. charge to   I ....   4. cheat   M....................

2. atone for   E ....   5. beg   I ....

3. stagnate   V....................

X. Check the correct definition or synonym.

1. *facilitate*
   a. make better   b. make easier   c. make happier
2. *emulate*
   a. imitate   b. deny   c. question
3. *gesticulate*
   a. use gestures   b. use words   c. use sounds
4. *plagiarize*
   a. steal literary   b. torture   c. attack
   property
5. *patronize*
   a. cater to   b. defer to with   c. cater to with
   with con-   respect   hesitation
   descension

XI. Write the required Greek or Latin stem and give one example of its use.

	Stem	Example
1. one	....	....
2. write	....	....
3. God	....	....
4. two	....	....
5. three	....	....

XII. Write in each of the five spaces the word that is defined.

1. Pathological incendiarism ....

2. Fear of closed spaces ....

3. Sleep-walking ....

4. Hostility to father, with undue attachment to mother ....

5. Delusions of persecution ....

XIII. Check the proper word.

1. *Loss of memory*
   a. insomnia   b. somnambulism   c. amnesia

2. *Incessant
   drunkenness*
   a. pyromania   b. kleptomania   c. dipsomania

3. *Troubled with
   imaginary ills*
   a. claustro-   b. acrophobia   c. hypochondria
   phobia

4. *Delight in
   inflicting pain
   on another*
   a. sadism   b. cynicism   c. iconoclasm

5. *Pandering to
   the passions of
   people to gain
   political power*
   a. anarchism   b. jingoism   c. demagoguery

XIV. Match the two columns by placing the appropriate
    letter of column B next to each word in column A.
    We have added an extra word in column B to make
    it more difficult.

	A.		*B.*
1.	disciplinarian	....	a. coquette
2.	bootlicker	....	b. egotist
3.	beginner	....	c. martinet
4.	conceited fellow	....	d. sycophant
5.	flirt	....	e. atheist
			f. tyro

XV. Proceed as in group XIV.

	A.		*B.*
1.	coin-collector	....	a. virtuoso
2.	one with good taste		b. philologist
	in food	....	c. philatelist
3.	beauty worshiper	....	d. numismatist
4.	student of language	....	e. gourmet
5.	skilled artist	....	f. esthete

XVI. Proceed as before.

	A.		*B.*
1.	man with one wife	....	a. ornithologist
2.	seer	....	b. ethnologist
3.	eye-doctor	....	c. clairvoyant
4.	dabbler in art	....	d. oculist
5.	student of birds	....	e. monogamist
			f. dilettante

XVII. Write in the word that will pair off with its synonym or definitive phrase.

1. drowsiness or indifference   L ....
2. full to repletion   S ....
3. exhausted   E ....
4. boredom   E ....

5. haughtily contemptuous   S ....

XVIII. Write down the meaning of each of the following Greek stems.

1. anthropo   ....

2. poly   ....

3. philo   ....

4. miso   ....

5. theos   ....

XIX. Pair off the words in these two columns.

A.		*B.*
1. taciturn	....	a. learned
2. esthetic	....	b. tireless
3. loquacious	....	c. satisfyingly beautiful
4. indefatigable	....	d. talkative
5. erudite	....	e. silent

XX. Write down the word whose meaning and initial letter are given.

1. Minor indiscretion P ....
2. Boastfulness B ....
3. Complicated and embarrassing situation I ....
4. War-mongering J ....
5. To shirk work by pretending illness M ....

XXI. Match the words in these two columns.

A.		B.
1. introvert	....	a. truculent
2. inhibited	....	b. one whose mind is turned inwards
3. diffident	....	c. quixotic
4. with impractical ideals	....	d. shy
5. overbearing	....	e. frustrated

XXII. Check the correct antonym, or word with a meaning that is opposite to the meaning of the italicized word.

1. *plebeian*
   a. common   b. ordinary   c. distinguished
2. *inane*
   a. wise   b. necessary   c. useful
3. *wanton*
   a. hopeful   b. restrained   c. lovely

4. *obsequious*
   a. brusque   b. happy   c. sad
5. *crass*
   a. rapid   b. refined   c. good

XXIII. Match the words of same or similar meaning in
       these two columns:

	A.		B.
1.	carelessly	....	a. adroitly
2.	skillfully	....	b. vociferously
3.	sourly	....	c. irascibly
4.	smoothly	....	d. glibly
5.	loudly	....	e. cursorily

XXIV. From the list at the end of this section (XXIV),
      find an antonym or antonymic phrase for each of
      the following and write it in its correct place.

1. miscegenation   ....
2. esoteric   ....
3. nebulous   ....
4. moribund   ....
5. scurrilous   ....

useless	solid	necessary
known to all	satisfactory	stingy
marriage with one's	healthy	wavering
own race	wasteful	respectful

XXV. From the list at the end of this section (XXV) pick a synonym or a synonymic phrase for each of the following words, and write it in its proper place.

1. parsimonious ....

2. catholic ....

3. uxorious ....

4. profligate ....

5. chauvinistic ....

imaginary	liberal	object of hatred
hater of women	wasteful	desirable
stingy	homesickness	tireless
over-patriotic	excessively fond of one's wife	well-meaning

XXVI. Write "same" or "opposite" next to each pair of words that follow, wherever the meanings are "the same" or "opposite."

1. analogous, similar ....

2. ambiguous, clear ....

3. epigrammatic, pointless ....

4. euphemistic, crude ....

5. redundant, repetitious ....

XXVII. Write down the meaning of each of these italicized stems.

1. dips*omania*   ....

2. *bi*ped   ....

3. *tri*pod   ....

4. *pod*ium   ....

5. bi*cycle*   ....

XXVIII. Write down the meaning of each of these italicized stems.

1. *anim*ate   ....

2. *bene*fit   ....

3. *fac*tory   ....

4. *dic*tate   ....

5. *uni*te   ....

XXIX. Each one of the following five words is followed by a definition. Where the definition is correct, write down "yes"; where it is incorrect write "no."

1. ochlocracy   ....   rule by a dictator

2. omniscient   ....   all-knowing

3. fetish   ....   object of hate

4. facet   ....   hope

5. abstemious   ....   gluttonish

XXX. Write "true" or "false" next to each statement, according to whether it is correct or incorrect.

1. Chimerical things are tangible. ....

2. Machiavellian people are naïve. ....

3. Pariahs are popular. ....

4. Diffident people are generally
   peremptory. ....

5. Querulous wives are happy. ....

ANSWERS:

You have just taken 30 tests including a total of 155 questions. Each question correctly answered should count 2 in your favor. A perfect score would then be 310. Please check your results against the following answers and add up your total. Compare your marks with the following table.

Excellent 250-310

Good 200-250

Fair 100-200

Poor 0-100

I. 1-b; 2-a; 3-b; 4-a; 5-b

II. dipsomania, megalomania, pyromania, kleptomania, bibliomania, egomania, nymphomania, anglomania, francomania

III.   1-rusticate; 2-procrastinate; 3-deprecate; 4-ostracize; 5-scintillate

IV.   1-oculist or ophthalmologist; 2-pediatrician or pediatrist; 3-psychiatrist; 4-dermatologist; 5-orthodontist

V.   1-feet; 2-women's diseases; 3-skin diseases; 4-eye diseases; 5-delivery of babies

VI.   1-c; 2-a; 3-a; 4-c; 5-b

VII.   1-atheism; 2-agnosticism; 3-egoism; 4-epicureanism; 5-chauvinism

VIII.   1-history of mankind; 2-rocks; 3-ancient relics or excavations; 4-unborn animals or children; 5-insects; 6-history of races; 7-derivation of words; 8-birds; 9-language; 10-human mind

IX.   1-impute; 2-expiate; 3-vegetate; 4-mulct; 5-importune

X.   1-b; 2-a; 3-a; 4-a; 5-a

XI.   1-mono (monocle, monogram, monologue, monomania)
2-graph (graphology, autograph, graphic)
3-theo (theology, theocracy, monotheism)
4-bi (biped, bicycle, bicuspid)
5-tri (triangle, tricycle, tripod)

XII.   1-pyromania; 2-claustrophobia; 3-somnambulism; 4-Oedipus complex; 5-paranoia

XIII.   1-c; 2-c; 3-c; 4-a; 5-c

XIV.   1-c; 2-d; 3-f; 4-b; 5-a

XV.   1-d; 2-e; 3-f; 4-b; 5-a

XVI.   1-e; 2-c; 3-d; 4-f; 5-a

XVII.   1-lethargy; 2-satiated; 3-enervated; 4-ennui; 5-supercilious

XVIII.   1-man; 2-many; 3-love; 4-hate; 5-God

XIX. 1-e; 2-c; 3-d; 4-b; 5-a

XX. 1-peccadillo; 2-braggadocio; 3-imbroglio; 4-jingoism; 5-malinger

XXI. 1-b; 2-e; 3-d; 4-c; 5-a

XXII. 1-c; 2-a; 3-b; 4-a; 5-b

XXIII. 1-e; 2-a; 3-c; 4-d; 5-b

XXIV. 1-marriage with one's own race; 2-known to all; 3-solid; 4-healthy; 5-respectful

XXV. 1-stingy; 2-liberal; 3-excessively fond of one's wife; 4-wasteful; 5-over-patriotic

XXVI. 1-same; 2-opposite; 3-opposite; 4-opposite; 5-same

XXVII. 1-craze; 2-two; 3-three; 4-foot; 5-wheel

XXVIII. 1-mind or spirit; 2-well; 3-do, make; 4-say, tell; 5-one

XXIX. 1-no; 2-yes; 3-no; 4-no; 5-no

XXX. 1-false; 2-false; 3-false; 4-false; 5-false

A LIFETIME HABIT

In one sense you have finished this book. In another we hope you have just begun.

You have, perhaps, learned to know many words more intimately. And *any* new word that you learn in your life will add amazingly to your power to think. Once a man thinks—really thinks—he has little competition. You may remember that the Irish playwright George Bernard Shaw one time said that few people think more than two or three times a year. He claimed that he had made an international reputation by thinking as often as once a week! And please remember that there is no expedient to which a man will not resort to avoid the labor of thinking.

It will be more important now than ever before to shine up all the instruments in your kit that may prove to be the tools to success. We are coming out into a tough and tangled world. Those who are well equipped will survive. Those who are not, may not. In almost every life, in every age, one gets what one asks for, and in this age of all others there will be very few alibis allowed.

There is not much of a secret to success. It is a great thing that is usually won by humble, routine methods. The mere decision you made to begin these chapter lessons was an important step, for, as the Chinese say, "The journey of a thousand miles begins with a single step."

So continue with your word study. Watch for new words at all times. Never be content until you know the meaning of a strange one. Make it your own possession. Use it in a letter, in conversation. List it in your pocket notebook, with its common meaning, its pronunciation, and a sentence in which it is used. Have a little mental rehearsal on these words now and again while you are walking along the street. Carry on an imaginary conversation.

An intelligent argument, by the way, will give your new words a real workout. In such a challenge, a sharply accurate knowledge of the exact meanings of words is invaluable. But you should learn *how* to argue, if you don't already know. And most people *don't* know. They are apt to think with their emotions and not with their minds. And they deal in generalities and not with facts. If you will keep cool and *choose your words,* you will have a great advantage. Before you start, be sure that you and your opponent are arguing about the same thing. There are certain so-called ghost-words like *Communist, United Nations, Democracy, Neutrality, Freedom of Speech,* that are vague and nebulous and may mean totally different things to different people. It is futile for you and your friend to debate about the U.N. unless you have both first *defined* the words and decided precisely what each of you understands them to mean. To you, your idea of the U.N. may seem to offer salvation for the future; and to your friend, according to the way he understands the words, the whole thing may be anathema. You will find it amusing and interesting as a parlor game to have each one present write down his or her definition of such ghost-words as United Nations or Communism. No two definitions will be alike and therefore any argument on such subjects will spin around in unprofitable circles.

Use such methods as these to test and try your words. You will find your powers getting stronger and stronger.

We can take particular and patriotic pride in mastering our speech. For ours is no longer the English language. It is the American language. Our language is as different from so-called English as South American Spanish is from the Castilian Spanish of Spain.

As a matter of fact there is no true "English" language, as Scotland, Ireland and Wales, and the various departments of England itself all have their dialects. The Lincolnshire farmer and the Lancashire miner can't even understand each other. England, like almost every other nation in the world, is a mass of discordant dialects.

What we know as the "English" language is, much more truly, the "London" language and a particular part and class of London at that, as the inhabitants of Limehouse might laugh at the cockney dialect and the taxidriver would smile at the toff.

So there is every reason why we should take a deep and passionate pride in the American language. It has a beautiful unity throughout our land. No other country in the world, one tenth our size, can show such linguistic solidarity, nor any approach to it. This American language is our creation; it belongs to us, and the more we master it, the more secure we will make our democracy.

INDEX
and
PRONUNCIATION KEY

PRONUNCIATION KEY

On the following pages are listed all of the words that have been studied in this volume, together with their proper pronunciations. *The Funk and Wagnalls New Standard Dictionary*, 1940 Edition, has been used as the authority.

KEY	ILLUSTRATIVE WORDS
ä	as in artistic, cartoon.
ä	as in art, cart, alms, father.
ă	as in at, add, fat, man, lap, baffle.
â, ê	as in air, fare, pear, heir, there.
ĕ	as in get, bell, says, leopard, said, dead, bury, added.
ā, ę	as in prey, wait, fame, great, neighbor.
ĭ, ў	as in hit, tin, miss, cyst, physic.
ē, ĭ, ў	as in police, mete, greet, sea.
o	as in obey, poetic, window, photo.
ō	as in go, note, glory, blow, soul, goat, beau.
ŏ, ạ	as in not, odd, what, was.
ô, ạ	as in or, north, all, haul, walk.
u̇, ọ, ŏŏ	as in full, push, could, stood.
ṳ, ọ, ōō	as in rule, true, food, who, lose.
ŭ, ó	as in but, under, son, other.
û, ê, ĭ, ȳ	as in burn, cur, earn, whirl, myrrh.
ī, ў	as in aisle, pine, sign, light, type, height.
ou, ow	as in sauerkraut, out, now.
ū	as in duration, futility.
ū	as in feud, tube, pupil, beauty.
ŏi, ŏy	as in oil, coin, boy, oyster, loyal.
k, c	as in kin, cat, back, ache, pique, quit.
g	as in go, dog, egg, ghost, guard.
ṇ, ng	as in sing, long, ringing, link.
th	as in thin, bath, faith, ether, Luther.
th	as in this, with, breathe, rather, either.
s, ç	as in so, house, this, missing, cent, scene, psychology.
z, ẓ	as in zest, lazy, buzz, was, houses.
ch	as in chin, rich, church, watch.
j, g̣	as in jet, gin, gist, judge, pigeon.
sh, çh	as in ship, dish, issue, nation, ocean, function, machine.
zh	as in azure, seizure, leisure, vision.
á	as in ask, chant, dance, fast.
a, e, o, u	as in sofa, final, about, over, separate, mystery, guttural, martyrdom (always unstressed).
a, e, i, u, y	as in habit, senate, surfeit, biscuit, minute, menace, average, privilege, valley, Sunday, cities, renew (always unstressed)

INDEX

256